Oral Training Course

口语实训教程

（上册）

主编　陶长安
编委　刘晖　陶然
　　　（美）Jason Tang

中国科学技术大学出版社

内 容 简 介

《口语实训教程》注重英语口语表达特点和会话交际能力,分为上、下两册。上册分为前后两部分:Lesson 1~16 旨在训练学生英语单词发音、句子连读、段落意群和口语语速等基本技能,纠正学生错误的英语发音习惯,使学生能够初步构筑语篇,进行基本对话;Lesson 17~32 通过拓展学生国际视野,进行综合会话训练,让学生能够流畅表达观点,达到与听话者进行自由会话、交流和讨论的目的。

教程根据我国设置的"中国英语能力等级量表",将内容与国家英语口语标准结合起来。其中,上册内容相当于"中国英语能力等级量表"三级,适合我国初、高中学生使用。

图书在版编目(CIP)数据

口语实训教程. 上册/陶长安主编. —合肥:中国科学技术大学出版社,2020.3
ISBN 978-7-312-04606-3

Ⅰ.口… Ⅱ.陶… Ⅲ.英语—口语—教材 Ⅳ.H319.9

中国版本图书馆 CIP 数据核字(2019)第 204561 号

出版	中国科学技术大学出版社 安徽省合肥市金寨路96号,230026 http://press.ustc.edu.cn https://zgkxjsdxcbs.tmall.com
印刷	合肥宏基印刷有限公司
发行	中国科学技术大学出版社
经销	全国新华书店
开本	787 mm×1092 mm 1/16
印张	8.75
字数	224 千
版次	2020 年 3 月第 1 版
印次	2020 年 3 月第 1 次印刷
定价	36.00 元

Foreword
前　言

　　《口语实训教程》分为上、下两册。上册共32课,可供具有初中及以上水平的学生使用,即相当于"中国英语能力等级量表"的三级水平。下册共32课,可供具备高中及以上水平的学生使用,即相当于"中国英语能力等级量表"的四级水平。

　　通过本册的学习,学生可以打下良好的英语基础,同时对亚洲和非洲国家有一定的了解。在本册的学习过程中,学生可以:① 习得英语口语的基础知识;② 做到舌位灵活、语音清晰、语调恰当,并有强烈的意群意识;③ 英语表达基本准确、连贯、顺畅;④ 理解日常生活中常见的、简单的语言材料,获取关键信息,抓住要点,推断他人的意图;⑤ 在日常生活或一般社交场合中能用简单的语言与他人交流,描述个人经历、志向等。

　　下册通过某些侧面介绍西方主要国家,使学生对欧洲、美洲和大洋洲国家与联合国有一个大致的了解。通过下册的学习,学生可以:① 理解一般社交场合中常见话题的语言材料,能抓住主题和主要内容,把握主要事实与观点,清楚他人的意图和态度;② 在熟悉的场合能就熟悉的话题进行对话,叙述事件发展,描绘事物状况,介绍相关活动,说明事物要点,简单论述个人观点等,且表达较为准确、清晰、连贯。

　　本书内容涉及工业、农业、商业、教育、外交、证券、房地产、旅游等。编者虚构了哈利和波特这两个角色,课文中许多他们的对话场景是编者在近50个国家和地区的见闻以及在各地学习、生活和工作的经历,以对话、独白、书信和演讲等方式和大家分享,用身临其境的方式让学生了解各地人文和自然景观,让学生在不同语境下学会英语表达技巧。

　　本书按照安徽省人社厅的要求,由合肥蓝鲸职业培训学校组织专家编写,既可以作为英语口语教材,也可以作为英语口语爱好者学习用书,特别适合准备出国旅游、留学和工作的人士使用。

　　2008年,编者在出席美国波特兰州立大学举办的世界翻译学大会时,受北京外国语大学王克非教授的委托做小组总结发言,受到好评。王教授希望编者将在世界各地的见闻落实成文字,编者几经推敲,用近6年的时间完成本书,谨此向王教授表示衷心的感谢。在撰写过程中编者得到了东南大学梁为祥教授、南京财经大学肖辉教授、哈佛大学许灵玥和马里兰大学吕秋蕊等同仁的支持,在此一并感谢!

编 者

2018 年 6 月

Contents

Foreword ·· (ⅰ)

Lesson 1　Coming to Know Each Other ································ (1)

Lesson 2　English Culture ··· (5)

Lesson 3　School Life ··· (9)

Lesson 4　Pronunciation ·· (13)

Lesson 5　Shopping ·· (18)

Lesson 6　Do Me a Favor, Please ·· (22)

Lesson 7　English and Englishes ··· (26)

Lesson 8　Tear Down ··· (30)

Lesson 9　Linked-sounds and Sense Group ····························· (34)

Lesson 10　Holidays ·· (38)

Lesson 11　Fast-food Industry ·· (42)

Lesson 12　A Better Way of Teaching English ······················· (46)

Lesson 13　Tongue-twisters ··· (50)

Lesson 14　Did You Hear What I Heard? ······························ (54)

Lesson 15　A New Story of the Hare and Tortoise (1) ············· (58)

Lesson 16　A New Story of the Hare and Tortoise (2) ············· (62)

Lesson 17　Chinese Dream ·· (66)

Lesson 18　Japan: a Place of Sunrise ··································· (70)

Lesson 19　Republic of Korea: a Place for Plastic Surgery ……………………（ 75 ）

Lesson 20　Israel: a Dynamic Nation for Startups ……………………（ 79 ）

Lesson 21　Malaysia and Malay ……………………（ 83 ）

Lesson 22　Angkor to Revive ……………………（ 87 ）

Lesson 23　Singapore: a City of Lion ……………………（ 91 ）

Lesson 24　A Visit to the Bali Island ……………………（ 95 ）

Lesson 25　ASEAN ……………………（ 99 ）

Lesson 26　Turkey: the Crossroad of East and West ……………………（103）

Lesson 27　Mysterious Dubai ……………………（107）

Lesson 28　League of Arab States ……………………（111）

Lesson 29　Moonlighting ……………………（116）

Lesson 30　South Africa ……………………（120）

Lesson 31　Namibia: the Youngest Country in Africa ……………………（124）

Lesson 32　Shanghai Cooperation Organization ……………………（129）

Lesson 1 Coming to Know Each Other

★ Making friend with an Australian boy at the Bondi Beach in Sydney.

Background Information

A friend in need is a friend indeed. Everybody tries to develop his or her relations with the people around so that they may get help from their friends. Therefore, learning how to share with other people is an important part of life, particularly, in the era of internet plus. Friendship counts and people need to team up to complete a certain kind of task or mission, and we believe cooperation help create win-win situation.

In a narrow sense, no one wants to be alone when they really want to do something big if you have pals. Two heads are better than one as is known to all.

In a broad sense, nothing is stronger than teamwork. Therefore, to be a team player is very important in life. Your mission can hardly be completed with the lack of friendship even though you have a great vision. Anyway, good relationships help to create positive energy rather than negative energy. More friends mean more resources you can use in the world today.

Lesson 1 Coming to Know Each Other

Ⅰ. Dialogue

Harry: Hello, Porter. Long time no see. What's up?

Porter: Hi, buddy. How come you are here at the party? Tell me where you've been to these years?

Harry: Well. After finishing my elementary school, I joined a boarding school in Nanjing, a private middle school. A few days ago, I completed my high school. And now I'm ready to go to a precollege in the States.

Porter: How time flies! You never realize that the time has passed so quickly. Let me show you some of my pals here.

Harry: Good idea. It seems that you are smiling to the girl with teased hair on the corner.

Porter: Nope. But the boy next to her. I mean the one with crew cut, in red T-shirt with black and white stripes. He is my cousin, called Adam. He is a name-dropper.

Harry: He looks like a baseball player.

Porter: Yes, he loves all sorts of sports like soccer and rugby, sometimes, basketball and fencing ...

Harry: Awesome! A real athlete. How often does he play sports?

Porter: He never plays sports. He only watches them on TV. He is quite a couch potato.

Harry: Interesting. Can I have the honor to know him?

Porter: Why not? Let me introduce ...

Ⅱ. New Words and Expressions

1. elementary [ˌelɪˈmentrɪ] *adj.* 基本的；初级的

2. boarding [ˈbɔːdɪŋ] *n.* 寄宿

3. private [ˈpraɪvət] *adj.* 私人的；秘密的

4. complete [kəmˈpliːt] vt. 完成;结束

5. realize [ˈrɪəlaɪz] vt. 意识到;实现

6. tease [tiːz] vt.& vi. 取笑;戏弄;梳理(羊毛)

7. crew cut n. 平头

8. stripe [straɪp] n. 条纹

9. name-dropper [ˈneɪm drɒpə] n. 狐假虎威的人

10. introduce [ˌɪntrəˈdjuːs] vt. 介绍;引进

11. rugby [ˈrʌgbi] n. 橄榄球运动

12. fencing [ˈfensɪŋ] n. 剑术;围墙

13. awesome [ˈɔːsəm] adj. 令人敬畏的;极好的

14. couch potato n. 电视迷;整天看电视的人

15. honor [ˈɒnə(r)] n. 荣誉;光荣

Ⅲ. Exercises

Answer the following questions according to your knowledge:

1. Usually, how do people come to know each other in your country?

2. What kind of sports do they love to play?

3. How much do you know about the American football? Share with the class about how it is played.

4. Describe a person you know well and introduce him or her to your best friend.

Lesson 2 English Culture

★ Mr. Gorge is having a real time lecture on English literature at a historical site in Edinburgh, Scotland.

Background Information

Thanks to England's influential position within the United Kingdom, sometimes it can be hard to differentiate English culture from that of the United Kingdom as a whole. Its culture covers architecture and gardens, art, cuisine, folklore, literature, music, performing arts and religion. Many great writers were from England, such as William Shakespeare, William Wordsworth, the Bronte sisters, Francis Bacon.

Apart from scotish whisky, we all know Wimbledon, the Championships, a lawn tennis tournament, one of the four Grand Slam Championships. Sports and leisure are very popular in the U.K. and many of the sports we play today were given birth there, such as cricket matches, football or soccer, horse-racing and golf as well as many others.

Lesson 2 English Culture

Ⅰ. Text

Very often, it is sports that put English people together. They love sports in four seasons no matter spring, summer, fall or winter.

Golf is from Edinburgh, Scotland. Cricket is a royal game. Football or soccer and rugby are more teamwork. Tennis can be on singles or doubles. To play or not to play, that is the question.

Historically, England had some great writers like William Shakespeare, Francis Bacon and many others. Today, literature is a success for England with the Harry Potter series.

England's success of rock and pop music makes music an important part of English culture. It is a good place for music lovers.

Ⅱ. New Words and Expressions

1. sport ［spɔːt］ n. 体育运动；乐趣

2. put ... together 拼；组成整体

3. no matter 不论；不管

4. golf ［gɒlf］ n. 高尔夫球

5. cricket ［ˈkrɪkɪt］ n. 板球；蟋蟀

6. royal ［ˈrɔɪəl］ adj. 国王的；王室的；高贵的

7. game ［geɪm］ n. 比赛；游戏

8. rugby ［ˈrʌgbɪ］ n. 橄榄球

9. teamwork ［ˈtiːmwɜːk］ n. 团队

10. single ［ˈsɪŋgl］ adj. 单一的；（比赛）单打的

11. double ［ˈdʌbl］ adj. 双的；（比赛）双打的

12. writer ［ˈraɪtə］ n. 作家

13. literature ［ˈlɪtərətʃə］ n. 文学；文学作品；文献；著作

14. success ［səkˈses］ n. 成功，成就

15. series ［ˈsɪəriːz］ n. 系列

16. rock ［rɒk］ n. 摇滚乐

17. pop music ［pɔp ˈmjuːzɪk］ n. 流行音乐

18. culture ［ˈkʌltʃə］ n. 文化；文明

19. place ［pleɪs］ n. 地方

20. health ［helθ］ n. 健康

Ⅲ. Exercises

Answer the following questions according to your knowledge：

1. What is the most popular spectator sport in England?
2. How much do you know about the Big Ben and Westminster? Share your understanding of these two majestic buildings with your peers.
3. Which English writer do you know best? Why?
4. What kind of English song do you like best?

Lesson 3　School Life

★ Students in London use buses to go to school instead of traveling by school bus.

Background Information

Schooling is a vital process of human beings. The high level of cultural education decides the leading position on science and technology all over the world. In America, most people experience nursery, kindergarten, preschool, elementary school, middle school, high school, precollege, college and university. Everyone has an opportunity to receive systematic education and develop personal talent and abilities as well as skills.

Elementary equals to primary and primary means important and fundamental. Therefore, the education of elementary school is true primary and is the most important part of the educational system across the world. First of all, the students are expected to know something of general situation through the primary school education system. In the U.S., primary school education is mainly managed by education committee of each particular state and local governments. In most systems, education is divided into three parts: six years for primary school, three years for junior high school, and another three years for senior high school. Nine years compulsory education is conducted in many countries.

After junior high school, most of the students may choose to go to a vocational school to learn a trade while others will continue their academic program.

Ⅰ. Dialogue

Harry: I take subway to go to school. How about you?

Porter: Well, I travel by school bus. Usually, I have a light breakfast so that I have more time for sleeping.

Harry: Unlike you, I spend a lot of time enjoying my heavy breakfast.

Porter: This is why you like metro. I hear it's crowded, like sardine.

Harry: Yes, but time-saving. How do you like your school life?

Porter: It's ok. But my English teacher is great. He always lets me know something that is not in the book.

Harry: What's your favorite class?

Porter: I like Physical Education best. By the way, how do you go home? By bus or bike share?

Harry: Actually, my parents pick me up sometimes. Once in a while, I go home on foot.

Porter: That's great!

Harry: What time are you free from school?

Porter: At 17:30, but I do hope it's one o'clock like in the west. And then the school bus will take me home.

Harry: It's cool to be on a roller coaster or Ferris wheel on weekends. A ride on London Eye is always my dream.

Porter: No wonder after-school life is more interesting.

Ⅱ. New Words and Expressions

1. use [juːs] *vt.* 使用;运用
2. subway [ˈsʌbweɪ] *n.* (美)地铁;地下通道
3. travel [ˈtrævl] *vt.& vi.* 游历;旅行;经历

4. light ［laɪt］ *adj*. 轻的；少量的

5. unlike ［ˌʌnˈlaɪk］ *prep*. 不像；（表示属性）与……不同

6. heavy ［ˈhevɪ］ *adj*. 重的；大量的

7. metro ［ˈmetrəʊ］ *n*. （欧洲）地铁

8. crowded ［ˈkraʊdɪd］ *adj*. 过于拥挤的；挤满的

9. sardine ［ˌsɑːˈdiːn］ *n*. 沙丁鱼；庸碌无能的人

10. time-saving ［taɪm ˈseɪvɪŋ］ *adj*. 节省时间的；省时的

11. physical ［ˈfɪzɪkl］ *adj*. 身体的；自然界的；物质的

12. education ［ˌedʒuˈkeɪʃn］ *n*. 教育；教育学

13. bike share *n*. 共享单车

14. pick up *v*. 捡起；用车接某人

15. once in a while 偶尔；时不时

16. free from （把……）从……释放出来；使摆脱

17. roller coaster *n*. 过山车

18. Ferris wheel *n*. 摩天轮

19. ride ［raɪd］ *n*. 乘骑；（乘车）旅行

20. dream ［driːm］ *n*.& *vt*. 梦；梦想；做梦

21. no wonder 难怪；怪不得

Ⅲ. Exercises

Answer the following questions according to the dialogue：

1. Why does Harry go to school by subway?

2. Do you agree that a math teacher shares the knowledge of social science in the class with his or her students?

3. What class does Porter like? And what does Harry like?

4. What are your hobbies? Why?

Lesson 4 Pronunciation

★ Translators and interpreters are meeting at UN's Geneva Office and pronouncing the same words in their own mother tongue.

Background Information

Some Chinese students are timid when they speak to foreigners partly due to their concern of mispronunciation. Therefore, a good pronunciation will enable you to communicate your ideas clearly. As an English saying goes, "Good beginning is half the battle". So spending some time on twisting your mouth on regular basis is worthwhile and rewarding. In this way, you will speak proficient English, and others will better understand what you say as well.

Actually, pronunciation is not a big trouble for Chinese students if you follow the instructions provided in this text. Of course, what is described in the text is not enough at all. You need to improve the articulation and utter each of the phonetics correctly. In terms of speaking American English or English English, it is up to your choice, but it seems that more and more students tend to do American English. In the author's eyes, pronunciation is only a small thing but remember that small things make big difference in the learning of a foreign language. Also what matters is your accent. And what you can do is to pay attention to using the right part of your tongue and get rid of accent, got it?

Lesson 4 Pronunciation

I. Dialogue

Harry: Hi, Porter. It's fine today, but I don't feel fine just because of my homework.

Porter: Why? You just look happy in the class.

Harry: Well. Every time I try to pronounce a particular word I have to face the music, for instance, everybody does "very well", but I do "wery well".

Porter: I see, you don't want to invite trouble, do you? Remember it's "very well", not "wery well".

Harry: You'd better not to trouble the trouble till the trouble troubles you. But it seems to me "very well" and "wery well" are the same.

Porter: Nope. When you do "v", you should use your upper teeth to touch your lower lip.

Harry: Ok. Let me have a try. Wery, very, wery, very, very, very ...

Porter: You made it!

Harry: Many of my classmates have the similar problem. Instead of saying "thank you", they do "sank you".

Porter: You are right. The right way to pronounce "th" is to use your tongue tip to slightly touch your teeth when you pronounce it.

Harry: I got it and I really appreciate you.

Porter: No big deal. It's because you never use that part of the tongue, I think.

Harry: I have a Chinese pal whose last name is Tao. The foreigners always call him "Mr. Yao" or "Mr. Dao", but never "Tao". Now I understand why their accent is weird.

Porter: I give it two thumbs up as your pronunciation is becoming more like it. Remember teachers are teachers. I do the right things, you do things right.

Harry: One more story about the pronunciation is that some Chinese utter "n" as "l". For example, can I use your life? It will frighten the westerners.

Porter: Actually, he or she means "Can I use your knife?" this time.

Ⅱ. New Words and Expressions

1. pronounce [prəˈnaʊns] v. 发音

2. face the music 直面困难；承担后果

3. for instance 例如

4. invite [ɪnˈvaɪt] vt. 邀请；招致

5. remember [rɪˈmembə] v. 记住

6. seem [siːm] vi. 似乎

7. upper [ˈʌpə(r)] adj. 上部的

8. lower [ˈləʊə(r)] adj. 下部的

9. lip [lɪp] n. 嘴唇

10. instead of 代替

11. slight [slaɪt] adj. 轻微的

12. tongue [tʌŋ] n. 舌头

13. touch [tʌtʃ] vt. 接触；联系

14. deal [diːl] n. 处理，交易

15. foreigner [ˈfɒrɪnə] n. 外国人；陌生人；外来物

16. accent [ˈæks(ə)nt; -sent] n. 口音

17. weird [wɪəd] adj. 奇怪的

18. thumb [θʌm] n. 大拇指

19. frighten [ˈfraɪtn] vt.& vi. 吓走；惊恐；使害怕

20. utter [ˈʌtə(r)] vt. 讲；说；发出声音

Ⅲ. Exercises

Answer the following questions according to your knowledge:

1. Practice more words with "th" and "s" or "th" and "z", or "v" and "w".

2. Find more tongue-twisters to exercise, such as: the weather doesn't know whether the weather is like the weather.

3. Find more words to tell the differences between "n" and "l".

4. Did you encounter the same problem in the pronunciation? If so, tell us when?

Lesson 5 Shopping

★ A pedestrian street for shoppers on weekends in Sydney, Australia.

Lesson 5 Shopping

Background Information

In the west, people bought things through barter trade at the beginning. With the appearance of money, they started to purchase things from a grocery store. Then they began to buy things in a bigger place, called department store. In 1960s, Americans started to shop in a supermarket with the advent of plastic card. In 1980s, people in the U.S. believe it is a good idea to put department stores under the same roof, hence a shopping mall was born. A shopping mall enables more buyers to do one-stop shopping and get almost everything. You can also enjoy recreational activities in the shopping mall. The consumers who like to shop in a mall are called mall rats. Are you a mall rat? Or just a window shopper?

Nowadays, various brand-new ways are popular, such as category shopping, TV shopping, online shopping, are widely accepted. Which do you prefer?

Ⅰ. Dialogue

Harry: How often do you go shopping?

Porter: Every day. But I never shop in the physical shop like a grocery store, department store, supermarket or a shopping mall.

Harry: Then, how do you get things? In a virtual shop?

Porter: Well, I use a computer or mobile phone to buy, and I never use cash. All I need to do is to Open my WeChat Pay or Alipay. It is really cool to shop online.

Harry: I only purchase food in the physical shop, for example, grains, fruits, French fries ... And I pay with my credit card.

Porter: We call French fries as potato chips. The more potato you eat, the more you look like a couch potato. By the way, are you a veggie?

Harry: Not really. Instead, I can eat a horse and I love lamb and steak. Sometimes sandwich and hot-dog, particularly hamburger. And usually I finish my dinner with chocolate or ice cream.

Porter: That is not healthy. Do you know the Food Pyramid?

Harry: Never heard of it.

Porter: Now let me tell you ...

Ⅱ. New Words and Expressions

1. physical ['fɪzɪkl] *adj.* 物理的；实体的
2. grocery ['grəusərɪ] *n.* 食品杂货店
3. mall [mɒl] *n.* 大型购物中心；购物广场
4. virtual ['vɜːtʃuəl] *adj.* （计算机）虚拟的
5. mobile phone *n.* 手机；移动电话
6. cash [kæʃ] *n.* 现金
7. prepay ['priː'peɪ] *vt.* 充值

8. grain [greɪn] n. 谷粮

9. credit card n. 信用卡

10. online [ˌɒn'laɪn] adj. 在线的；网上开通的

11. the more ... the more ... 越……越……

12. veggie ['vedʒɪ] n. 素食者

13. steak [steɪk] n. 牛排

14. healthy ['helθɪ] adj. 健康的

15. finish ... with ... 以……结束……

16. particularly [pə'tɪkjələlɪ] adv. 尤其；特别地

17. pyramid ['pɪrəmɪd] n. 金字塔

18. never heard of it 没听说过；闻所未闻

19. as well as conj. 以及；和

Ⅲ. Exercises

Answer the following questions according to the dialogue：

1. What is Porter's way of shopping?

2. What food does Harry buy in the shop?

3. What is the way of your shopping?

4. Group up and talk about the Food Pyramid.

Lesson 6   Do Me a Favor, Please

★ A volunteer is helping others prune ivy at a castle in Switzerland.

Lesson 6　Do Me a Favor, Please

Background Information

A prince is a male member of a royal family, especially a son of the king. A crowned prince is the child of a royal family who is to be the next king or queen. Sometimes, prince can be a noble man of varying rank and status or a person of high rank or of high standing in his class or profession. A princess is a member of a royal family who has sovereign power or a female member of a royal family.

In some families, kids are very independent and know how to make pocket money by helping their parents with housework, but in other families, we may see an opposite view. It seems that some children love to give order and their parents or grandparents just take order, which is pretty much a concern for the nation.

Human beings are social animals, and we play different roles in our communities. Helping one another is not abnormal. It is worth mentioning that one turn deserves another. If we spoil our kids too much, we will never know what is going to happen tomorrow. It is time to take a close look at our educational system for kids. The earlier, the better.

Ⅰ. Dialogue

Harry：How often do you help your parents at home?

Porter：Never. They don't need my hand. They believe I can only create troubles for them rather than help them.

Harry：When I wanna tidy my bed myself every morning, my mother normally says I am too young to do it.

Porter：Usually I would love to water the flowers in the yard but my grandpa says it is his work. It's really cool to see him sweeping the floor on his knees.

Harry：Sometimes, I help my dad to wash the dishes, but my grandma says I am a little prince. She tells me not to do that ...

Porter：My aunt says a little princess never does that either.

Harry：By the way, can you do me a favor? Can you help me to set the table now?

Porter：Sure! I am good at dusting the furniture and I am doing fast too.

Harry：That's a piece of cake for me because I have a robot bought by my dad to help me make some pocket money. I love the pocket money but easy come, easy go.

Porter：Actually we can help our parents a lot, but in their eyes, we can do nothing ...

Harry：Being the only child in the family, I can not do whatever I want.

Porter：Me too. However, I know they stopped the one birth control policy few years ago. I am pretty much concerned about my future.

Ⅱ. New Words and Expressions

1. favor ['feɪvə] n. 好感；关切
2. create [kriːˈeɪt] v. 创造；发明
3. rather than 而不是；宁可……也不愿
4. wanna [ˈwɒnə] v. = want to（美俚）想；要
5. tidy [ˈtaɪdɪ] v. 整理

6. too ... to ... 太……而不能够

7. young [jʌŋ] adj. 年幼的；有朝气的

8. yard [jɑːd] n. 院子；场地

9. sweep [swiːp] v. 打扫；扫除

10. knee [niː] n. 膝；膝盖

11. set [set] v. 安置；使处于某种状况；设置；摆放餐具

12. dust [dʌst] n. & v. 灰尘；拂（一拂），掸（一掸）

13. furniture [ˈfɜːnɪtʃə] n. 家具

14. prince [prɪns] n. 王子；（某些欧洲国家的）贵族

15. princess [ˌprɪnˈses] n. 公主

16. actually [ˈæktʃuəlɪ] adv. 实际上

17. do sb. a favor 给某人帮助

18. be good at 善于做某事

Ⅲ. Exercises

Answer the following questions according to the dialogue:

1. Please pronounce each particular word in the text and make sure your pronunciation is well-uttered.
2. What do Harry and Porter often do at home?
3. What attitude do their parents take towards their doing housework?
4. Are you the only kid in the family? What do you usually do to help your parents?

Lesson 7 — English and Englishes

★ Buckingham Palace is the place where Queen's English is spoken.

Lesson 7 English and Englishes

Background Information

English is the language of England, the U.S. and many areas of former British colonies. English comprises English language, literature or so. Englishes refer to the English language used by the people out of England.

The issue of World Englishes was first raised in 1978 to examine concepts of regional Englishes globally. Pragmatic factors such as appropriateness, comprehensibility and interpretability justified the use of English as an international and intra-national language. In 1988, at a Teachers of English to Speakers of Other Languages (TESOL) conference in Honolulu, Hawaii, the International Committee of the Study of World Englishes (ICWE) was formed. In 1992, the ICWE formally launched the International Association for World Englishes (IAWE) at a conference of "World Englishes Today", at the University of Illinois, USA. There is an academic journal devoted to the study of this topic now, titled World Englishes.

Currently, there are approximately 75 territories where English is spoken either as a first language (L1) or as an unofficial or institutionalized second language (L2) in fields such as government, law and education. It is difficult to ascertain the total number of Englishes in the world, as new varieties of English are constantly being developed and discovered.

I. Dialogue

Harry: Hi, Porter, it's quite a while since we met last time. You speak very good English now.

Porter: Yes, I do. I am speaking to you in English and my "bruda" also speaks good English.

Harry: Are you talking to me in English? You speak English English or American English?

Porter: I speak neither English English nor American English. I speak Indian American English.

Harry: What's that? Can you tell me the differences? I am a bit puzzled.

Porter: Well, English English means London English. People in Scotland, Wales and Ireland speak their own language respectively, like Scottish, Welsh and Irish.

Harry: Do most people in Scotland, Wales and Ireland speak English?

Porter: Yes, they do. And Indian American English is American English used by the Indian Americans.

Harry: Are you mentioning American Indian?

Porter: No. I mean Indian Americans and American Indians in America like those in the Silicon Valley rather than those aborigines like American Indians in the reserve.

Harry: I hear there are Australian English, Kiwi English, Canadian English, and Egyptian English. So people speak World Englishes.

Porter: What is World Englishes?

Harry: World Englishes is a special term for emerging localized or indigenized varieties of English, especially varieties that have developed in territories influenced by the United Kingdom or the United States. By the way, what does "bruda" mean?

Porter: Well, actually it is brother, but with Indian accent.

Lesson 7 English and Englishes

Ⅱ. New Words and Expressions

1. neither ... nor ... 既不……也不……
2. Scotland ['skɒtlənd] n. 苏格兰(在大不列颠岛北部)
3. Wales [weɪlz] n. 威尔士(英国的一部分)
4. Ireland ['aɪələnd] n. 爱尔兰(岛)
5. language ['læŋgwɪdʒ] n. 语言；语言文字
6. respectively [rɪ'spektɪvlɪ] adv. 各自地；各个地；分别地
7. silicon ['sɪlɪkən] n.〈化〉硅；硅元素
8. valley ['vælɪ] n. 山谷；谷地
9. emerge [ɪ'mɜːdʒ] vi. 出现；浮现；暴露
10. localize ['ləʊkəlaɪz] vt. 使局部化；使具地方色彩
11. territory ['terətrɪ] n. 领土；版图；领地；领域；范围
12. indigenize [ɪn'dɪdʒənaɪz] vt. 使本地化；使本国化
13. accent ['æksent] n. 重音；口音

Ⅲ. Exercises

Answer the following questions according to the dialogue：

1. What is the meaning of English English?
2. What language do Indians speak?
3. What language do Australians speak? Why?
4. How many languages can you speak?

Lesson 8　Tear Down

★ The building amid is being torn down in Jerusalem, Israel, and the rest establishments are under restoration.

Background Information

Awarded the 1937 Pulitzer Prize, the novel titled *Gone with the Wind* was adapted as a film in 1939 — an achievement that won ten Academy Awards. A historical romance set in Northern Georgia during the Drama of the Civil War and Reconstruction years.

"Gone with the wind" is used to describe that something is gone and never come back again, like some buildings. Over the past decades, many buildings have been torn down.

With the urbanization drive going on, many old constructions have been taken down for better skyline. Unluckily, some of the historical sites and places of interests are flattened by bulldozers in the process of modernization. Average people complain about the acts committed by those scalpers who illegally deprive the rights of theirs. A country can be destabilized by these evil action of demolishment.

Ironically, some of buildings are not permitted by the government to be demolished were destroyed. To demolish or not to demolish, that is the question.

Ⅰ. Dialogue

Harry: Hi, Porter, long time no see, how are things there?

Porter: Oh, Harry? I haven't seen you for years. You used to be a naughty boy and now you are a handsome man.

Harry: Yeah, everything is changing here. The old houses are all gone. Gone with the wind.

Porter: Yes, they are no longer here. All the old houses were torn down by the government. We have a new city now. The only thing that doesn't change is change.

Harry: How do you like your new life here?

Porter: Not really. The urbanization drive goes too fast. They demolish too many houses. I love the small old village life rather than the city life. In the past we could visit each other and talk to one another anytime, anywhere. But now we don't know each other even if we are neighbors.

Harry: Sure. City people are city people. Everybody is a stranger to them. Is it called new normal?

Porter: Of course not. Do you happen to know the meaning of "concrete box"?

Harry: Of course. That is where we live now. An apartment is called a flat in England. We need more developments like housing project, condominiums and studios.

Porter: I wish they gonna tear down my school and rebuild it!

Ⅱ. New Words and Expressions

1. tear down [tɪə daʊn] vt. 拆除；撕毁

2. naughty [ˈnɔːtɪ] adj. 顽皮的；不听话的

3. change [tʃeɪndʒ] vt. 改变；变更

4. gone [gɒn] adj. 过去的；不存在了的；无可挽救的

5. no longer 不再

6. government ['gʌvənmənt] n. 政府；政体

7. city ['sɪtɪ] n. 城市；全市居民

8. urbanization [ˌɜːbənaɪ'zeɪʃn] n. 城市化

9. drive [draɪv] v. 驱动；驾驶 n. 驱动力；驱动器

10. demolish [dɪ'mɒlɪʃ] v. 拆毁；摧毁

11. visit ['vɪzɪt] vt.& vi. 访问；参观

12. neighbor ['neɪbə] n. 邻居

13. stranger ['streɪndʒə(r)] n. 陌生人

14. even if 即使；虽然

15. concrete ['kɒnkriːt] adj. 混凝土制的；有形的

16. new normal n. 新常态

17. stay [steɪ] vt.& vi. 停留

18. development [dɪ'veləpmənt] n. 住宅小区

19. housing project n. 经济适用房

20. condominium [ˌkɒndə'mɪnɪəm] n.（拥有所有权的）套房

21. studio ['stjuːdɪəʊ] n. 单室套

Ⅲ. Exercises

Answer the following questions according to the dialogue：

1. Please pronounce each particular word in the text and make sure your pronunciation is well-uttered.

2. Do Porter and Harry see each other on regular basis? What changes have happened in the small old village?

3. What is your comment on the large scale demolishment?

4. How do you look at the current urbanization drive? Do you think it is necessary?

Lesson 9 Linked-sounds and Sense Group

★ Doing a simultaneous interpretation at an international conference in the UN needs to twist your mouth on the regular basis in the the whole process of meeting.

Lesson 9 Linked-sounds and Sense Group

Background Information

Some people speak English fluently thanks to the contribution of right pronunciation and linked-sounds. Others can't make it due to the lack of training. We believe a well-designed training program of pronunciation and linked-sounds is the precondition of your proficiency of speaking English.

Oral English is useful today because the foreigners are just around us in our daily life. Therefore, the right use of your tongue is very fundamental and will enable you to speak good English.

If correct pronunciation guarantees your listening and speaking ability of English, the linked-sounds guarantee your sense group. In this way you will be able to integrate yourself into English media soon.

Ⅰ. Dialogue

Harry: Porter, I have a friend who speaks such fluent English that you just can't tell if he is a Chinese or an American.

Porter: That's what's happening around us.

Harry: It's mind-boggling. I am all ears.

Porter: You know when we communicate with a foreigner, we understand him or her mostly. But when foreigners are talking to one another, we miss a lot of information. One of the reasons is that they use linked-sounds a lot.

Harry: What's a linked-sound? Any example to prove?

Porter: Sure. Within a word, if one consonant comes after the other, the one before will be silent or half silent. For instance, sandwich, in this word, "d" is silent. Another example, kept, this time "p" is half silent.

Harry: Ok. I really appreciate you. You've made it crystal clear. How about linked-sounds in between the words?

Porter: The same thing. Like 'talk to', in this phrase, "k" is half silent. Remember the linked-sounds must be done within a sense group of a sentence. By the way, a sentence may have several sense groups.

Harry: How about a consonant followed by a vowel then?

Porter: You hit the nail on the head. Because a vowel is the most often used part of English language, it appears anytime, anywhere. When the last word ends up with a consonant and followed by another word that starts with a vowel, you simply put them together, but within a sense group. For instance, good evening, "d" and "e" are linked.

Harry: I got it. Another thing that puzzles me during my learning is that the stress of a word or a sentence.

Porter: Well, I will share with you next time round due to the time limit. We have much in common ...

Lesson 9 Linked-sounds and Sense Group

Ⅱ. New Words and Expressions

1. consonant ['kɒnsənənt] *n*. 辅音
2. fluent ['fluːənt] *adj*. 流利的；熟练的
3. mind-boggling ['maɪndˌbɒglɪŋ] *adj*. 难以置信的
4. information [ˌɪnfə'meɪʃn] *n*. 信息；情况
5. reason ['riːzn] *n*. 原因；理由
6. prove [pruv] *v*. 证明；说明
7. silent ['saɪlənt] *adj*. （语）不发音的；沉默的
8. appreciate [ə'priːʃieɪt] *v*. 点赞；欣赏
9. crystal clear *adj*. 清晰的
10. phrase [freɪz] *n*. 短语
11. sense group *n*. 意群
12. vowel ['vaʊəl] *n*. 元音
13. stress [stres] *n*. 重音，强调
14. common ['kɒmən] *adj*. 普通的，相同的

Ⅲ. Exercises

Answer the following questions according to the dialogue：

1. Pronounce each particular word in the text and then try to link them up in a sense group.
2. Read the text again to find out the linked-sounds and practice in the class.
3. Most of the things that you want to know are never in the books that teach you English. How many sense groups in this sentence?
4. What is sense group? Underline the sense groups in the text and practice.

Lesson 10 Holidays

★ People are busy preparing activities for the upcoming Halloween.

Background Information

A holiday is a day set aside by custom or by law on which normal activities, especially business or work, are suspended or reduces. Generally, holidays are intended to allow individuals to celebrate or commemorate an event or tradition of cultural or religious significance.

Some holidays are celebrated world-wide while others are nation-wide or region-wide. Thanksgiving Day — a day appointed for giving thanks for divine goodness, the fourth Thursday in November observed as a legal holiday in the U. S.; the second Monday in October observed as a legal holiday in Canada.

The word *holiday* comes from the Old English word which originally referred only to special religious days. In modern use, it means any special day of rest or relaxation, as opposed to normal days away from work or school.

One can learn a lot about a particular country's tradition and custom via the observation of holiday celebration. The art of observation is to observe without being observed, so try to be a good observer.

Ⅰ. Dialogue

Harry: What day is today? It seems it is a big one, isn't it?

Porter: Yeah! It is the Independent Day in the States. The U.S. National Day is on July fourth. How about in China?

Harry: China celebrates it on October First. In China, apart from those solar calendar holidays, the Chinese have some lunar calendar holidays too, for example, Tomb Sweeping Day, Dragon Boat Festival and Moon Cake Festival or Mid-Autumn Day. In these days, China's free ways are all for free.

Porter: Interesting! In the States, Americans have many national holidays too, such as Christmas and New Year's Day, Good Friday, Easter, Veterans Day, Thanksgiving Day, etc.

Harry: In terms of celebration, they have some in common. Uncle Sam marks Halloween like the Ghost Day in China, and Veteran Day is something like the Double Nine Day. Unlike the west, the Valentine's Day falls on July seventh of lunar calender in China.

Porter: I notice that some holidays are popular, for instance, Father's Day, Mother's Day, Fool's Day as well as Valentine's Day.

Harry: How do you mark these events? I just know something of everything while you know everything of something.

Porter: Firework celebrations are held in many cities across the nation on the Independent Day like Spring Festival but no couplets. The sharing of a turkey dinner on Thanksgiving Day, etc.

Ⅱ. New Words and Expressions

1. seem [siːm] vi. 似乎；像是

2. independent [ˌɪndɪˈpendənt] adj. 自主的；独立的

3. celebrate [ˈselɪbreɪt] vt. 庆祝；歌颂

Lesson 10 Holidays

4. solar ['səʊlə(r)] adj. 太阳的；日光的

5. calendar ['kæləndə] n. 日历；历法

6. lunar ['lunə] adj. 月亮的；阴历的

7. traditional [trə'dɪʃənl] adj. 传统的；惯例的

8. tomb [tu:m] n. 坟墓；墓穴

9. dragon ['drægən] n. 龙

10. festival ['festɪvl] n. 节日；节期

11. mid [mɪd] adj. 中间的；居中的

12. free way [fri: weɪ] n. 〈美〉高速公路

13. free [fri:] adj. 自由的；免费的；免税的

14. veteran ['vetərən] adj. 有作战经验的；老兵的

15. ghost [gəʊst] n. 鬼，幽灵

16. eve [i:v] n. 前夜

17. double ['dʌbl] adj. 双的；两倍的

18. for instance 例如；比如

19. Easter ['i:stə(r)] n. 〈宗〉复活节

20. firework ['faɪəˌwɜ:k] n. （常 pl.）烟火，烟花

21. turkey ['tɜ:kɪ] n. 火鸡；蠢货

Ⅲ. Exercises

Answer the following questions according to the dialogue：

1. Which festivals are the most interesting ones in the U.S.A.?

2. Which festivals are there in China?

3. What is your favorite festival? Why?

4. Describe a traditional Chinese festival and share the way you celebrate with your team.

Study Notes

Lesson 11 Fast-food Industry

★ Fast-food brings convenience for people at having a meal.

Background Information

McDonald's is the world's leading fast-food chain with 32,000 restaurants worldwide. But now fast-food industries in China have been vigorously developing, which save much time and provide convenience for people in daily life and work.

Every cloud has its silver lining and there are always two sides to everything. Fast-food focuses on calories rather than nutrition and it is called junk food in the west. We are here to promote food pyramid. Try this healthy way of eating and you will rerecord the life expectancy.

Some kids love to go to a KFC or McDonald's and they may never ask for a receipt after their parents pay for the meal. In the States, if they fail to give your the receipt, you get a free meal in any of the fast-food restaurant.

Ⅰ. Dialogue

Harry: I don't have enough time for the buffet at the Grand Hyatt Hotel. Let's have some coffee, instead.

Porter: But, I'm really hungry. Why don't we go eating something just simpler?

Harry: I suppose we could. I have a very important meeting in one hour. Where could we go that is convenient?

Porter: How about KFC or McDonald's?

Harry: I prefer KFC. I do have an appetite for their chicken burger and a bowl of mashed potatoes.

Porter: Just give me a large order of French fries and I will be happy.

Harry: KFC has some new spicy chicken wings. You can choose from a selection of three different sauces. Let's see, there's sweet and sour, hot and spicy, and barbecue flavor.

Porter: We could order several chicken wings along with cola. Maybe even some chicken nuggets.

(Harry and Porter are sitting down in the KFC outlet.)

Harry: Wow! That was fast. It only took about two minutes to fill our order.

Porter: That's why they call it "fast-food". You still have half an hour to get to your meeting.

Harry: Still have time for that coffee.

Ⅱ. New Words and Expressions

1. French fries n. 法式炸土豆条
2. chicken burger n. 鸡肉汉堡
3. mashed potato n. 土豆泥
4. chicken wing n. 鸡翅
5. spicy ['spaɪsɪ] adj. 辣的

6. barbecue ['bɑːbɪkjuː] n. 烧烤
7. nugget ['nʌgɪt] n. 块
8. outlet ['aʊtˌlet] n. 商店
9. fast-food ['fɑːst 'fuːd] n. 快餐

Ⅲ. Exercises

Answer the following questions according to your knowledge:

1. Is there any fast-food outlets in your hometown?
2. Why is it that fast-food is quite convenient?
3. What do you want to eat in fast-food restaurant?
4. How much do you know about food pyramid?

Lesson 12 A Better Way of Teaching English

★ Teachers are encouraging the students to make a public speech.

Lesson 12 A Better Way of Teaching English

Background Information

Being a good English teacher, one needs to be bilingual first. It is also crucial to meet the minds of his or her students in order to convey the right information for the right people in a right place. There is a cultural difference between the two languages and we know clearly that behind the language lies the culture.

As for the methodology, ways have been explored. Such as Grammar-translation approach, Audio-lingual approach, total physical response, the direct method, the communicative approach, community language teaching, task-based language teaching, content-based instruction teaching, etc. Some believe task-oriented method is ideal while other may choose teacher-centered or student-centered way, diagram-based, and even translatology method. Some believe cognitive approach should be encouraged in the class while others are practising up to second perspectives, like problem-based learning or hackathon.

Anyway, different ways for different students are applied in the class. There is no best way, but a better way in teaching English.

Ⅰ. Speech

Morning, my fellow teachers. It's my honor to have you here. This is Harry speaking. What I am gonna share with you is my thoughts on how to work with students.

Well, in my eyes, the most important step is making friends with your students. The ideal relationship between teachers and students should be friendly, because friends can support each other, help each other and talk about almost everything they meet. No matter how classroom go on, we should keep asking if the students accept it or not.

English, as you know, is unfamiliar to Chinese students. Any negative stimulation from their teacher can dampen the enthusiasm of the students. As a result, it will surely lead to failure of teaching, so how to get on well with the students is always a question on the table. I think, from the very beginning, teachers should make friends with them. Any of your kind words, smiling face, gentle actions will make them feel as warm as spring, and shorten the distance between teachers and students. When they don't do English well, give them close care. When they meet difficulties in the process of learning, give them encouragement and help them build up their confidence. When they gain success, praise them at once.

We know it's easier said than done but we also do trust "Well begun is half done" and "Where there is a will there is a way".

Ⅱ. New Words and Expressions

1. step [step] n. 步骤;措施
2. ideal [aɪˈdiːəl] adj. 理想的
3. support [səˈpɔːt] vt. 支持;维持
4. almost [ˈɔːlməʊst] adv. 几乎;差不多
5. accept [əkˈsept] vt. 接受;承认

6. unfamiliar [ˌʌnfəˈmɪliə(r)] adj. 不熟悉的；陌生的

7. negative [ˈnegətɪv] adj. 消极的；(数)负的

8. stimulation [ˌstɪmjʊˈleɪʃn] n. 刺激；激发

9. dampen [ˈdæmpən] vt. 使……沮丧；抑制

10. enthusiasm [ɪnˈθjuːziæzəm] n. 热情；热忱

11. result [rɪˈzʌlt] n. 结果

12. lead to 导致；(道路)通向

13. failure [ˈfeɪljə(r)] n. 失败；不及格

14. gentle [ˈdʒentl] adj. 温和的；文雅的

15. action [ˈækʃn] n. 行为；手段

16. difficulty [ˈdɪfɪkəlti] n. 困难；难度

17. process [ˈprəʊses] n. 过程；做事方法

18. build up 建立；增进

19. confidence [ˈkɒnfɪdəns] n. 信心；信任

20. gain [geɪn] vt. 获得；增加

21. praise [preɪz] v. 赞扬；赞美

Ⅲ. Exercises

Answer the following questions according to the speech:

1. What is your way of teaching? How do you like it?

2. What is the author's method of teaching English?

3. Describe a teaching method that you are familiar with in the class and organize a class discussion to see which method is more accepted by the students.

4. What is hackathon? How much do you know about it?

Lesson 13　Tongue-twisters

★ Making tongue-twisters at an international conference on the translation and interpretation study in Portland State University, U.S.A..

Background Information

Tongue-twister is an expression that is difficult to articulate clearly. It is a lot of work to use the right part of the tongue. Also tongue-twisters will help to improve your speaking speed which allows you to convey more information within the given time.

It is a good idea for our students to make tongues flexible. Taking full advantage of the opportunities of speaking English is an important part of our learning a foreign language.

The author of this book strongly recommend you to learn the song *The Court of King Caractacus*. Weeks later, your tongue will be more flexible. Its lyrics is "Now the ladies of the harem of the court of King Caractacus, were just passing by ..."

Weather — a state of the atmosphere with respect to heat or cold, wetness or dryness, calm storm, clearness. The British are used to talking about weather first when they meet each other. It is a habit and common topic of the British.

Ⅰ. Dialogue

Harry：How do you like the weather?

Porter：Well, everybody talks about the weather, but nobody does anything about it.

Harry：Yeah. The weather doesn't know whether the weather is like the weather. By the way, do you sell shells?

Porter：Nope. But my sister Alice does, and she sells sea shells at the sea shores.

Harry：How much do you know about a woodpecker?

Porter：Just a little bit. And I know you know what I know is what you know.

Harry：How little then? Do you happen to know how much wood would a woodpecker peck if the woodpecker could peck wood?

Porter：That's your cup of tea.

Harry：Not really, I only know that a cup of tea remembers me.

Porter：Buddy, that's a good rhyming. Do you like this knife?

Harry：I don't like this knife but I do like the knife that I have.

Porter：Would you like to go swimming with me? Do you think you will sink in the water?

Harry：I think I will sink and you do think I will sink too. One more question, can you can the can?

Porter：No wonder it's a piece of cake for me to can the can.

Ⅱ. New Words and Expressions

1. tongue-twister [tʌŋ 'twɪstə] n. 拗口的句子（或表达）；绕口令
2. whether ['weðə(r)] conj. 是否
3. sell [sel] vt.& vi. 卖；出售
4. shell [ʃel] n. （贝、卵、坚果等的）壳；外壳
5. shore [ʃɔː] n. 岸；滨
6. woodpecker ['wʊdpekə(r)] n. 啄木鸟

7. happen ['hæpən] vi. 发生;碰巧;出现;偶然遇到

8. That's your cup of tea. 那是你的拿手好戏。

9. remember [rɪ'membə(r)] vt.& vi. 记得;牢记

10. buddy ['bʌdɪ] n. 密友,好友

11. rhyming ['raɪmɪŋ] n. 押韵

12. sink [sɪŋk] vt. 使下沉;使下垂

13. can [kæn] vt. 将……装入密封罐中保存 n. 罐头

14. no wonder 不足为奇

15. a piece of 一块;一片

Ⅲ. Exercises

Answer the following questions according to the dialogue:

1. Please practice the song *The Court of King Caractacus*. Weeks later, your tongue will be more flexible.

2. How many tongues-twisters do you know? Would you like to share some with you classmates?

3. Find more tongue-twisters and work your tongue, twist your mouth and make it more flexible.

Lesson 14 Did You Hear What I Heard?

★ Have you ever heard that Switzerland is a land of milk and honey with its picturesque view of countryside?

Background Information

At present, most people use computers for working, chatting, playing games, shopping, watching the movie or pictures, and searching for anything by clicking on internet.

The internet is a platform which allows us to collect all kinds of information we need. The right way of using your computer enables you to learn more than average people.

The author travels a lot to collect information for this book but come back home to see most of the things he wants just online. He believes that the more you see, the more you know and the more you know, the smarter you are. As the saying goes, "The art of observation is to observe without being observed".

The philosophical sentences in the text are part of the collections from both the author's traveling experiences and internet.

Ⅰ. Dialogue

Harry: Hi, buddy! Did you hear what I heard?

Porter: Well, I heard many funny sentences. Every time I eat out, my grandma's classical sentence will always come to me, "Look! you buy what you eat and eat what you buy".

Harry: Likewise, each time I shop online, my mother often tells me, "If you don't have what you like then you like what you have".

Porter: Good reminding. I remember my dad usually reminds me to be happy when I fail the exam.

Harry: What does he mean?

Porter: He says, "Happiness is wanting what you get and success is getting what you want". It sounds good to me.

Harry: Awesome! What does he mean exactly? Can you tell me a little bit about it?

Porter: Well, Let me share my knowledge with you. Sometimes I think he means if you fail to plan then you are planning to fail.

Harry: You seldom puzzle me, do you?

Porter: Actually, I am puzzled too.

Harry: Yeah, most of the things that you want to know are never in the books that teach you English.

Porter: I can't agree with you more.

Ⅱ. New Words and Expressions

1. classical [ˈklæsɪk(ə)l] *adj*. 经典的
2. likewise [ˈlaɪkwaɪz] *adv*. 同样地
3. remind [rɪˈmaɪnd] *vt*. 使想起,使记起;提醒
4. fail [feɪl] *vt.& vi*. 失败,不及格
5. exam [ɪgˈzæm] *n*. 〈口〉考试;测验

6. happiness ['hæpɪnəs] n. 幸福；高兴

7. success [sək'ses] n. 成功，成就

8. sound [saʊnd] vi. 响，发声；听起来

9. awesome ['ɔːsəm] adj. 令人敬畏的；极好的

10. exact [ɪg'zækt] adj. 准确的；严密的

11. mean [miːn] v. 意味着；产生……结果

12. plan [plæn] vt.& vi. 计划，打算

13. seldom ['seldəm] adv. 很少；罕见

14. puzzle ['pʌzl] vt.& vi. 为难；伤脑筋；使迷惑

15. agree [ə'griː] vt.& vi. 同意，赞同

Ⅲ. Exercises

Answer the following questions according to the dialogue：

1. What does Porter's father often tell him?

2. What does failure mean to Porter's father? What failure did you suffer usually in your daily life?

3. What attitude did you take when your failure happened?

4. What is your understanding of success and happiness?

Lesson 15 — A New Story of the Hare and Tortoise (1)

★ People are watching the race of hare and tortoise.

Lesson 15 A New Story of the Hare and Tortoise (1)

Background Information

Hare and Tortoise is a tale of the fable, which enlightens one, "Modest helps one to go forward, whereas conceit makes one lag behind". Honest and hard-working are the preconditions of doing anything, in this way one can make it.

Sticking to a good tradition is an important part of a culture, but never follow a stereotype routine and we should never judge a book by its cover. Remember everything is changing, some even change dramatically and the only thing that does not change is change. No one wants to be lagged behind in the race.

The definition of race is the classification of humans into groups based on physical traits, ancestry, genetics or social relations. It is also explained as a contest of speed. The upcoming two new stories of hare and tortoise is inspiring. It shows the creative life of our time, therefore keep thinking different.

I would love to share my thoughts with you that better late than never and never too old to learn. Keep momentum and remain learning for life time. It is always a good idea to start something new.

Past experience, if not forgotten, will guide the future. Hope you will enjoy the new story of the hare and tortoise.

Ⅰ. Text

Once upon a time, a tortoise and a hare had an argument about who was faster. They decided to settle the argument with a race. They agreed on a way and started off the race.

The hare shot ahead and ran quickly for some time. Then seeing that he was quite ahead of the tortoise, he thought he'd sit down under a tree for some time and relax before going on the race.

He sat under the tree and soon fell asleep. The tortoise plodding on overtook him and soon finished the race, emerging as unquestioned champ.

The hare woke up and realized that he'd lost the race.

He realized that he'd lost the race only because he had been over confident, and careless.

If he had not taken things for granted, there is no way the tortoise could have beaten him. So he challenged the tortoise to another race. The tortoise agreed.

This time the hare went all out and ran without stopping from start to finish. He won by several miles. But this is not the end of the story, there are more to see in the next episode.

Ⅱ. New Words and Expressions

1. hare [heə(r)] n. 野兔

2. decide [dɪˈsaɪd] vt. 决定；决心；解决

3. settle [ˈsetl] vt. 解决；安排；(使)定居

4. argument [ˈɑːrɡjumənt] n. 争论，争吵；论据

5. race [reɪs] n. 种，种族；(速度)比赛

6. agree [əˈɡriː] vt. & vi. 同意，赞同

7. shot [ʃɒt] n. 射手，击球；开枪

8. ahead of 提前

9. relax [rɪˈlæks] vt.& vi. (使)轻松;(使)松弛

10. fall [fɔːl] vi. 掉下,落下;下降 n. 降落,下降;瀑布;秋天

11. asleep [əˈsliːp] adj. 睡着的;休眠的

12. plod [plɒd] vt. 沉重地走

13. overtake [ˌəʊvəˈteɪk] vt. 追上,赶上

14. emerge [ɪˈmɜːdʒ] vi. 出现,浮现

15. unquestioned [ʌnˈkwestʃənd] adj. 不成问题的,无疑问的

16. champ [tʃæmp] vt. 大声咀嚼;冠军

17. lose [luːz] vt. 失去;错过

18. take for granted 认为……理所当然,想当然

19. beat [biːt] vt. 打败;敲打

20. challenge [ˈtʃæləndʒ] vt. 向……挑战

Ⅲ. Exercises

Answer the following questions according to the text:

1. Try to pronounce each particular word in the text correctly.

2. Do you hear of a tale about the race between a tortoise and a hare? Can you tell it in detail?

3. What does the hare realize in the end? Who won the race? Why?

4. What race does the tortoise figure out to challenge the hare?

Lesson 16: A New Story of the Hare and Tortoise (2)

★ The author is carefully studying the sea turtle in Indonesia and thinking of the nature of sea turtle.

Lesson 16 A New Story of the Hare and Tortoise (2)

Background Information

Peace and development are the common goal of human beings which is clearly described in the UN Charter. This is also the truth in the animal world. Today more and more people believe we can reach the goal through cooperation. Win-win situation is replacing zero-sum game in many areas including the international arena.

Just like the hare and the tortoise in this text, they may not reach the finishing line even they go all out and do the best like the tortoise. But they can achieve it when both of them have the same goal and maximize their own strength. We can conclude that cooperation is the growing trend of our times.

Ⅰ. Text

The tortoise thought for a while, and then challenged the hare to another race, but in a different way. The hare agreed. The hare took off and ran at top speed until he came to a broad river. The finishing line was on the other side of the river. The hare sat there wondering what to do. In the mean time, the tortoise trundled along, got into the river, swam to the opposite bank, continued walking and finished the race.

The hare and tortoise, by this time, had become pretty good friends and they did some thinking together. So they decided to do the last race again, but to run as a team this time.

They started off, and this time the hare carried the tortoise till the riverbank. There, the tortoise took over and swam across with the hare on his back.

On the opposite bank, the hare again carried the tortoise and reach the finishing line together. They both felt a greater sense of satisfaction than they'd felt earlier.

In life, when faced with failure, sometimes it's appropriate to work as harder and put in more effort. Sometimes it's appropriate to change strategy and try something different. And sometimes to do both.

The hare and the tortoise also learnt another a vital lesson. When we stop competing against a rival and instead start competing against the situation, we perform far better.

Ⅱ. New Words and Expressions

1. go all out   全力以赴;甩开膀子
2. take off   起飞;(使)离开
3. broad ［brɔːd］ *adj*. 宽的;辽阔的
4. side ［saɪd］ *n*. 面;边;方面;侧面
5. wonder ［ˈwʌndə］ *vt*. 对……感到好奇;想弄明白

6. trundle ['trʌndl] vt. 慢步走；迈着沉重的脚步走

7. decide [dɪ'saɪd] vt. 决定；决心

8. take over   接管；在……上花费

9. a sense of   有……的感觉

10. satisfaction [ˌsætɪs'fækʃn] n. 满足；满意

11. failure ['feɪljə(r)] n. 失败；不及格

12. appropriate [ə'prəʊprɪət] adj. 适当的；合适的

13. effort ['efət] n. 尝试；成就

14. strategy ['strætədʒɪ] n. 战略；策略

15. vital ['vaɪtl] adj. 有活力的；重要的

16. compete [kəm'pɪt] vt. 竞争；竞赛

17. situation [ˌsɪtʃu'eʃən] n. 情势；处境

18. perform [pər'fɔːrm] vt. 履行；运行；表现

Ⅲ. Exercises

Answer the following questions according to the text：

1. Why does the hare sit there wondering what to do?

2. How do you find that they become pretty good friends? What feeling do they have by this time?

3. How are people faced with it when they are confronting failure?

4. What is win-win situation? Set us an example.

Lesson 17 Chinese Dream

★ Bird's Nest in Beijing, the beginning of a life time dream.

Lesson 17 Chinese Dream

Background Information

Unlike American dream which is money and freedom, Chinese Dream combines personal benefit with the national interests closely. Chinese dream has started ever since the Opium War in 1840 when allied powers invaded China, as the Chinese president put it at the end of 2012 that China will regain its power and revitalize its economy from the year 2021 to 2049 in a step by step manner. This will be the golden period for the Chinese to realize their dream.

Since the founding of the the People's Republic of China in 1949, the ambitious Chinese have moved from the planned economy to market economy. Today China is open totally to the outside world and determined to materialize the great renaissance of the Chinese nation.

Ⅰ. Text

China is famous for the Four Great Inventions such as compass, paper-making, gunpowder and movable printing. The country attributes all these achievements to its education. When the education is on the right track, the inventions would come out.

The past experience, if not forgotten, will guide the future, as Confucius put it. What we need to do today is to better our education system so that people can know more about the world. The more education we have, the more fruit of inventions we enjoy. In this way, China will realize its dream ASAP. Close your eyes and imagine how important the education is. And China gives priority to its education. That is why some Chinese are learning in other countries or study abroad while others are busy sending spaceships to the moon. "Where there is a will, there is a way", as the English saying goes. We believe we will live a better life in a better city very soon.

Today, the Chinese people are working hard to realize the Chinese Dream. Everyone knows the Chinese saying, "You are not a true man until you get to the Great Wall". We believe, at present, the best way to realize Chinese Dream is the continuation of opening further to the outside world and reform to create a better atmosphere in an all round way for its development at various levels. And Go Global strategy will help China to find way out.

Ⅱ. New Words and Expressions

1. invention [ɪnˈvenʃn] n. 发明;发明物
2. compass [ˈkʌmpəs] n. 罗盘;指南针
3. gunpowder [ˈɡʌnpaʊdə(r)] n. 火药;有烟火药
4. movable [ˈmuːvəbl] adj. 活动的;可移动的
5. print [prɪnt] vt.& vi. 印刷;用印刷体写
6. attribute [əˈtrɪbjuːt] vt. 认为……是;把……归于
7. achievement [əˈtʃiːvmənt] n. 成就;成绩

Lesson 17 Chinese Dream

8. education ［ˌedʒuˈkeɪʃn］ n. 教育；教育学
9. track ［træk］ n. 小路；踪迹；轨道
10. past ［pɑːst］ adj. 过去的；以前的
11. guide ［gaɪd］ vt. 引路；指导；导游
12. future ［ˈfjuːtʃə］ n. 前途；未来
13. realize ［ˈriːəlaɪz］ vt. 实现；意识到
14. imagine ［ɪˈmædʒɪn］ vt. 设想；想象
15. important ［ɪmˈpɔːtnt］ adj. 重要的；权威的
16. believe ［bɪˈliːv］ vt. 相信；认为
17. send ［send］ vt. 发送；派遣
18. spaceship ［ˈspeɪsʃɪp］ n. 宇宙飞船
19. involve ［ɪnˈvɒlv］ vt. 包含；使参与；牵涉
20. construction ［kənˈstrʌkʃn］ n. 建筑物；建造；建设
21. The Belt and Road 一带一路

Ⅲ. Exercises

Answer the following questions according to the text：

1. What are the Four Great Inventions? Who was the first westerner that introduce them to the rest of the world?
2. How much do you know about China's educational system in the ancient times?
3. What is Chinese Dream?
4. Team up to discuss the differences between Chinese dream and American dream.

Lesson 18 Japan: a Place of Sunrise

★ Girls wearing Kimono in Kyoto, the former capital of Japan before Tokyo.

Lesson 18 Japan: a Place of Sunrise

Background Information

Japan is an island country in East Asia. Located in the Pacific Ocean, it lies to the east of the Sea of Japan, the East China Sea, China, Korean Peninsula and Russia, stretching from the Sea of Okhotsk in the north to the East China Sea. The kanji that make up Japan's name mean "sun origin", and Japan is often called the "Land of the Rising Sun".

Japan is an archipelago of 6,852 islands. The four largest ones are Honshu, Hokkaido, Kyushu, and Shikoku, which make up about ninety-seven percent of Japan's land area. Japan's population of 127 million is the world's tenth largest. Approximately 42 million people in Tokyo, the capital city of Japan, which is the second largest city in the OECD.

I. Dialogue

Harry: Hi, Porter. What have you been doing lately?

Porter: I went to Japan by a cruise called Costa Serena. It's quite a floating hotel. And I wanna share my experiences in the neighboring country with you.

Harry: Oh! I am all ears to hearing your story. How do you look at the Japanese culture?

Porter: Well, we have much in common in terms of culture. Thanks to the contribution of Mr. Jianzhen, a blind Chinese monk who had crossed the Sea for six times in the Tang Dynasty (618~907 A.D.) helped the Japanese to be creative.

Harry: Exactly. We drink tea in China while they do tea ceremony in Japan. We have flower arrangement while they do ikebana. We use rice as staple food while they do sushi. We enjoy rice wine while they do sake, etc.

Porter: Correct. The Japanese kimono is more or less like the costume of the Tang Dynasty. To be honest, I didn't feel I was in Japan because I could see so many Chinese characters here and there and I felt I was in China. You know, some 70 percent of Japanese characters are the same with the Chinese ones both in form and meaning.

Harry: Correct. You know, the westerners believe the word "bonsai" is originated from the Japanese. Actually it means potted-landscape, which is called "penzai" in China, a plant grow in a pot that is to be shaped and trimmed for scenery.

Porter: Anyway, the two countries have a lot of differences such as we drive on the right while they do the opposite; we have advertising on both sides of the freeway while they have none; we cook fish while they enjoy raw fish or sashime. We sleep in bed while they sleep on tatami or mattress.

Harry: What deserves our attention is that the streets are exceptionally clean and drivers strictly abide by the traffic laws.

Porter: Thanks to the Meiji Restoration which is an epoch-making event.

Lesson 18 Japan: a Place of Sunrise

Ⅱ. New Words and Expressions

1. cruise ［kru:z］ n. 游船；旅行

2. float ［fləut］ v. 漂浮；漂游

3. neighbor ［'neɪbə］ vt. 友好；毗邻而居

4. culture ［'kʌltʃə］ n. 文化；养殖

5. in terms of   至于……；谈及……；就……而言

6. monk ［mʌŋk］ n. 和尚；僧侣；修道士

7. dynasty ［'daɪnəstɪ］ n. 朝代；王朝

8. creative ［krɪ'eɪtɪv］ adj. 有创造力的；创新的

9. ceremony ［'serəmənɪ］ n. 仪式

10. ikebana ［ˌɪkɪ'ba:nə］ n. 花道

11. staple food n. 主食

12. sushi ［'su:ʃɪ］ n. 〈日〉寿司；生鱼片冷饭团

13. sake ［seɪk］ n. 日本清酒

14. kimono ［kɪ'məunəu］ n. 〈日〉和服

15. costume ［'kɒstju:m］ n. 戏装；(某地或某历史时期的) 服装

16. character ［'kærəktə(r)］ n. 汉字；特征；特点

17. bonsai ［'bɒnsaɪ］ n. 〈日〉盆景

18. trim ［trɪm］ vt. 修剪；整理

19. advertising ［'ædvətaɪzɪŋ］ n. 广告；广告业

20. exceptionally ［ɪk'sepʃənəlɪ］ adv. 异常地；特殊地

21. restoration ［ˌrestə'reɪʃn］ n. 修复

Ⅲ. Exercises

Answer the following questions according to the dialogue：

1. Pronounce each particular word in the text and then try to link them up in a sense group.

2. How did Perter travel to Japan? Did he find anything new?
3. Who is Mr. Jianzhen?
4. How much do you know about the Meiji Restoration?

Lesson 19: Republic of Korea: a Place for Plastic Surgery

★ A glimpse of downtown Seoul in the capital of Republic of Korea.

Background Information

The name of Korea comprises of two parts, "Ko" and "rea". "Ko" means "gao" in Chinese (the same as the Chinese character "高") while "rea" equals to "li" (equivalent to "丽"), hence Korea means "高丽" in Chinese. In this aspect, close your eyes and imagine, how close the ties between China and Korea can be.

Korea is divided into Democratic People's Republic of Korea and Republic of Korea on the Korean Peninsula geographically, which occupies very important position. Korean culture is really exciting right now. The Korean Wave is sweeping Asian countries including China. Young people are going crazy about Korean dramas and Korean pop songs.

Economically, Republic of Korea, together with Singapore, Chinese Hong Kong and Chinese Taiwan, are regarded as the Four Asian Tigers. This not so large country has made a great contribution to the global economy. The advertising of Sumsung and Hyundai can be seen here and there out of Republic of Korea.

Lesson 19 Republic of Korea: a Place for Plastic Surgery

Ⅰ. Text

Today, many people like to watch Korean TV series which are popular in China. Many of the plays are time-consuming and they may end up with a similar story: a man and a woman can not get married due to various reasons such as one of them dies or they are brother and sister but they did not know that before.

I like Republic of Korea not because of the play series but of the views. The views in Seoul, the capital of Republic of Korea, are not that impressive. However, in the Jeju Island, things are different. You can see many beautiful places with sands, sunshine and sea food. Some people go fishing there while others for views and relaxation only.

Shopping is attractive too. Travelers like to buy ginseng and pickles for souvenirs. Young Chinese people would love to purchase cosmetics and Korean fashions have many Chinese fans too. There are lots of DFS — Duty-free Shops which attract a lot of buyers. But tourism industry is always fragile, for example, the MERS cases have brought down the number of foreign visitors dramatically. And the tourist market suffers a lot due to many uncertain reasons.

It's interesting to see that almost every woman in Republic of Korea spend hours making up early in the morning. They believe their dressing up is to show respect to anyone they meet. Some ladies are fond of doing plastic surgery or cosmetic surgery and it's common in Republic of Korea.

Ⅱ. New Words and Expressions

1. series ['sɪərɪz] n. 系列;连续;(广播或电视)系列节目
2. consume [kən'su:m] vt. 消耗;消费
3. end up with 以……结束
4. view [vju:] n. 风景;景色;观点
5. relaxation [ˌrɪlæk'seʃən] n. 消遣;放松;松弛;放宽

6. attractive ［əˈtræktɪv］ *adj*. 有魅力的；引人注目的；迷人的

7. fashion ［ˈfæʃən］ *n*. 时尚；时装

8. traveler ［ˈtrævlə］ *n*. 旅行者；游客

9. ginseng ［ˈdʒɪnseŋ］ *n*. 人参

10. pickles ［ˈpɪklz］ *n*. 泡菜

11. souvenir ［ˌsuːvəˈnɪə］ *n*. 纪念品

12. purchase ［ˈpɜːtʃəs］ *n*. 购买

13. cosmetics ［kɒzˈmetɪks］ *n*. 化妆品

14. duty free *adj*. 免税的

15. tourism industry *n*. 旅游业

16. fragile ［ˈfrædʒaɪl］ *adj*. 易碎的；脆弱的

17. MERS = Middle East Respiratory Syndrome *n*. 中东呼吸综合征

18. dramatically ［drəˈmætɪklɪ］ *adv*. 戏剧性地；引人注目地

19. plastic surgery *n*. 整形手术

20. uncommon ［ʌnˈkɒmən］ *adj*. 不寻常的；罕见的

Ⅲ. Exercises

Answer the following questions according to the text：

1. Why are Korean TV series so popular in China? Are you taken to the Korean TV Series?

2. Why do many ladies go to Repulic of Korea for plastic surgery?

3. Can you talk about the views in Jeju Island?

4. What cause the tourist market sluggish in Repulic of Korea recently?

Lesson 20 Israel: a Dynamic Nation for Startups

★ The Western Wall (also called Wailing Wall) in Jerusalem, Israel.

Background Information

It shares land borders with Lebanon to the north, Syria in the northeast, Jordan on the east, the Palestinian territories comprising the West Bank and Gaza Strip to the east and west respectively, Egypt to the southwest, and the Gulf of Aqaba in the Red Sea to the south.

The notion of the "Land of Israel", known in Hebrew as *Eretz Yisrael*, has been important and sacred to the Jewish people since Biblical times.

With a population of 8.3 million, Israel boasts more than 5000 startups including 250 R & D centers such as Google and Microsoft. It's worth mentioning that the Israeli population takes up only 0.2% in the world but the Nobel Prize winners occupies 22%.

Lesson 20 Israel: a Dynamic Nation for Startups

Ⅰ. Text

Israel is a startup nation. It's very small in size but it's powerful in many areas.

Created in 1918 by Jewish celebrities like Albert Einstein, Sigmund Freud, Hebrew University of Jerusalem, ranking number one nationally and number 145 internationally, has produced 8 Nobel Prize winners. The university houses Einstein's manuscripts.

Israel's Innovation Eco-System is world famous and a visit to a leading startup company of its kind in Jerusalem will help you to understand in a better way of the secret of the Jewish Brain, connection between Judaism and innovation. By the way, dripping technology is widely applied. Farmers, occupying 5 percent of the total population, use this technology to provide food to 95 percent of the Israeli citizens.

Today people world over flock into Tel Aviv, the Israeli capital, to learn about the Entrepreneurship Spirit and Crowd Funding. Visiting a venture capital fund firm is always recommended to pay a visit to JVP, a venture capitalist focusing on cyber security, which had successfully secured the investment from China's Alibaba.

Ein Gedi Kibbutz is a collective community in Israel that was traditionally based on agriculture. It began as Utopian communities a combination of socialism and Zionism. It is here that people are equal and work together. All the properties belong to the collective.

You may also witness the ruins of Jaffa, which will bring you back to the history. The Wailing Wall makes you think a lot. Dead Sea Floating is unique in which one can read newspaper while swimming. Close your eyes and imagine why?

Ⅱ. New Words and Expressions

1. Israel ['ɪzreɪl] *n.* 以色列
2. startup ['stɑːtʌp] *n.* 创业；创新
3. celebrity [səˈlebrətɪ] *n.* 名人；名流；知名人士

4. rank [ræŋk] n.& vt. 等级;军衔;把……分等级

5. manuscript ['mænjuskrɪpt] n. 手稿;原稿

6. eco-system ['iːkəʊ 'sɪstəm] n. 生态系统

7. Judaism ['dʒuːdeɪzəm] n. 犹太教;犹太主义;(总称)犹太人

8. flock into 大批涌入;蜂拥而至

9. entrepreneurship [ˌɒntrəprə'nɜːʃɪp] n. 企业家的身份;职权

10. crowd funding n. 众筹;人群资助

11. venture capital n. 风险资本

12. recommend [ˌrekə'mend] vt.& vi. 推荐;建议

13. cyber security n. 网络安全

14. commune ['kɒmjuːn] n. 公社;亲密的会谈

15. secure [sɪ'kjʊə] vt. (使)获得;(使)安全

16. investment [ɪn'vestmənt] n. 投资;(时间、精力的)投入

17. equal ['iːkwəl] adj. 相等的;平等的

18. property ['prɒpətɪ] n. 财产;地产

19. collective [kə'lektɪv] n.& adj. 集体;集体的;共同的

20. Jaffa ['dʒæfə] n. 以色列雅法古城,意为"美丽"

Ⅲ. Exercises

Answer the following questions according to the text:

1. When was Hebrew University established? Who were the co-founders of the university?

2. What is a venture capital fund firm? Tell us something about crowd fund.

3. What is Kibbutz? Describe the life style of the people in the commune.

4. What do tourists do in Jerusalem? Name some of the tourist destinations.

Lesson 21 Malaysia and Malay

★ Petronas Twin Towers in Kuala Lumpur, the capital of Malaysia. It is called Menara Berkembar Petronas in Malay.

Background Information

Malay language or Bahasa Melayu, a major Austronesian language spoken in Malaysia, Indonesia, Brunei, and Singapore.

Old Malay, the Malay language from the 4th to the 14th century.

Malay languages, a group of closely related languages in the Malay Archipelago.

Malay trade and creole languages, a set of pidgin languages throughout the Malay Peninsula and Malay Archipelago.

Brunei Malay, an unofficial national language of Brunei distinct from standard Malay.

Kedah Malay, a variety of the Malaya languages spoken in Malaysia and Thailand.

Sri Lankan Creole Malay, a language spoken by the Malay ethnic minority in Sri Lanka.

Indonesian language, the official form of the Malay language in Indonesia.

Lesson 21 Malaysia and Malay

Ⅰ. Dialogue

Harry: Last time you mentioned that people in Malaysia and its neighbor countries speak Malay, right?

Porter: Yes. You are right. Do you speak Malay?

Harry: Just a little bit. I am still learning. It's challenging and I found it tough to learn.

Porter: As a matter of fact, it's not that difficult. Firstly, you are in Malaysia now, people around you can help you in many ways. Secondly, don't worry about making mistakes, but to learn from mistakes. Then try to use it often and it's everybody's knowledge that the best way to learn is to use.

Harry: How do you count one, two, three ... in Malay?

Porter: Satu, Dua, Tiga ... Easy, right?

Harry: Yes. I've learnt how to greet people and I know good morning is Selamat Pagi, good noon is Selamat Siang, Selamat Sore means good afternoon, and Selamat Malam equals good evening.

Porter: Hilarious! I give it two thumbs up.

Harry: Terima kasih! You improve a lot and you are really a quick learner.

Porter: I feel overpraised. Last time, I was trying to say goodbye to my peers in Malay, it seems that they were awkward when I said Makan to them.

Harry: In fact, Makan means eat, you are expected to say Sampai Jumpalagi.

Ⅱ. New Words and Expressions

1. mention ['menʃn] v. 提到;提及
2. neighbor ['neɪbə] n. 邻居;附近
3. challenge ['tʃæləndʒ] v. 挑战
4. tough [tʌf] adj. 困难的;硬的;难对付的
5. Satu(马来语)= one 一

6. Dua(马来语) = two 二

7. Tiga(马来语) = three 三

8. greet [gri:t] v. 问候;问好

9. Selamat Pagi(马来语) = good morning 早上好

10. Selamat Siang(马来语) = good noon 中午好

11. Selamat Sore(马来语) = good afternoon 下午好

12. Selamat Malam(马来语) = good evening 晚上好

13. equal [ˈiːkwəl] v. 等于;等同

14. hilarious [hɪˈleərɪəs] adj. 非常滑稽的;令人捧腹的

15. thumb [θʌm] n. 拇指

16. improve [ɪmˈpruːv] v. 提高;改善

17. overpraise [ˌəʊvəˈpreɪz] v. 评价过高;过奖

18. awkward [ˈɔːkwəd] adj. 难堪的;笨拙的

19. Makan(马来语) = eat 吃

20. expect [ɪkˈspekt] vt. 期望;预料;认为某事会发生

21. Sampai Jumpalagi(马来语) = good bye 再见

Ⅲ. Exercises

Answer the following questions according to the dialogue:

1. Pronounce each particular word in the text and then try to link them up in a sense group.

2. How to say one, two and three in Malay? Can you count down these numbers both in English and Malay?

3. What other words did Harry learn? Please name them in Malay.

4. Why do people feel awkward when Porter say Makan to the peers?

Lesson 22 Angkor to Revive

★ A panoramic view of the Angkor Wat in Siem Reap, Cambodia.

Background Information

In 802 A.D., Jayavarman II declared himself king marking the beginning of the Khmer Empire which flourished for over 600 years. The Indianized kingdom built monumental temples including Angkor Wat, now a World Heritage Site. After the fall of Angkor to Ayutthaya in the 15th century, Cambodia was then ruled by its neighbors. In 1863, Cambodia became a protectorate of France which doubled the size of the country by reclaiming the north and west from Thailand.

Cambodia has a population of over 15 million. The country gained independence in 1953 and faces numerous challenges including widespread poverty, pervasive corruption, lack of political freedoms, low human development, and a high rate of hunger.

Cambodia also faces environmental destruction as an imminent problem. The most severe activity in this regard is considered to be the countrywide deforestation, which also involves national parks and wildlife sanctuaries.

Lesson 22 Angkor to Revive

Ⅰ. Dialogue

Harry: Hello, Porter. I overhear you went to Cambodia lately. Is it right?

Porter: Correct. Views in Angkor are just marvelous.

Harry: How is the life in the country of rainforest? Are people living in a land of milk and honey?

Porter: Not really, to be frank, the country is relatively poor due to various reasons though it was prosperous for six centuries.

Harry: Yeah. In 802 A. D., Jayavarman II declared himself the king marking the beginning of the Khmer Empire which flourished for over 600 years.

Porter: The Vietnam War extended into the country with the U.S. bombing of Cambodia from 1969 until 1973 leading the war-torn country into deep water. But in my eyes, the country is picking up.

Harry: With the practice of China's Belt and Road Initiative, Cambodia is having more opportunities. It's time for the country to board China's economic train as a free rider.

Porter: Yes, we know Angkor Wat is being restored. More tourists are swarming into the kingdom.

Harry: A regional power, China's booming economy will enable Cambodia to be revitalized.

Porter: Sure. China's five principles of peaceful coexistence really benefit the surrounding countries a lot.

Ⅱ. New Words and Expressions

1. Angkor ['æŋkɔː] n. 吴哥
2. Cambodia [kæm'bəʊdɪə] n. 柬埔寨
3. rainforest ['reɪnfɔːrɪst] n.（热带）雨林
4. land of milk and honey n. 鱼米之乡

5. prosperous ['prɒspərəs] adj. 富裕的;繁荣的;兴旺的

6. Jayavarman Ⅱ n. 阇耶跋摩二世

7. Khmer Empire n. 高棉帝国

8. flourish ['flʌrɪʃ] vt. 兴旺;茂盛;繁荣

9. Vietnam [ˌvjet'næm] n. 越南

10. bomb [bɒm] n.& vt. 炸弹;炸毁

11. war-torn [wɔr tɔrn] adj. 饱受战争蹂躏的

12. pick up （商业）好转

13. Angkor Wat （柬埔寨）吴哥窟

14. free rider 搭便车者;免费享用公共货物者

15. restore [rɪ'stɔː] vt. 修复;归还;交还;使恢复

16. swarm [swɔːm] n.& vi. 一大群;涌入

17. booming ['buːmɪŋ] adj. 急速发展的

18. revitalize [ˌriː'vaɪtəlaɪz] vt. 复兴;复活;苏醒

19. principle ['prɪnsəpl] n. 原则;原理;准则

20. coexistence [ˌkəʊɪg'zɪstəns] n. 共存;共处

21. benefit ['benɪfɪt] vt. 有益于;有助于

Ⅲ. Exercises

Answer the following questions according to your knowledge:

1. How much do you know about Cambodia?

2. What are the five principles of peaceful coexistence?

3. Do you think that old kingdom is to be vitalized soon?

4. How do you look at China's Belt and Road Initiative and its impact on the surrounding countries?

Lesson 23 Singapore: a City of Lion

★ Singapore is also named Lion City.

Background Information

Singapore, an important member of the ASEAN and Commonwealth, is located to the south end of Malay Peninsula. The city state declared its independence from Malaysia in 1965. Economically, Singapore is one of the four tigers in Asia, overseas Chinese occupy 76% of its population, Malaysians constitute 15% who speak Malay language and English. Geographically, Malacca Strait is of great strategic importance.

The country is also noted for its petroleum refining, drilling construction in the sea, handling capacity of harbor, finance business and so on. There is almost no primary industry, but some secondary industry. Tertiary or third or service industry is well-developed. Anyway, Singapore holds important status in the world.

Lesson 23　Singapore: a City of Lion

I . Dialogue

Harry: Have you ever been to Singapore?

Porter: Yeah, I have been there for quite a few times, it is a garden city and a city state with nice people and beautiful sea views. Actually Singapore means a city of lion due to the visit of Alexander the Great according to the legendary story.

Harry: By the way, do Singaporeans speak English or Chinese?

Porter: Well, some 76 percent of Singaporeans are originally from China and they speak mandarin and Cantonese. The rest are from Malay and India as well as the west, and they speak their mother tongues.

Harry: Then what language do they use to talk to each other?

Porter: That is a good question. Singapore has four official languages: English, Malay, Mandarin Chinese and Tamil. English is the common language, and is the language of business, government, and the medium of instruction in schools.

Harry: Oh! I wish I could be there.

Porter: Good idea. If you speak English, it is a piece of cake for you to talk to each other. No worry about it, since you guys speak good English now.

Harry: Do they have good schools there? Like Zhuxi School.

Porter: Well, education in Singapore is number one. They have English schools and Malay schools as well as some Chinese schools. They also have boys' school and girls' school.

Harry: What can you do there?

Porter: Well, you can do a lot of things.

Harry: Can you give us some examples?

Porter: That's for sure. One of the highlights is Sentosa, where you can see the wildlife in the evening, like tiger and lion. You can also visit museums and golf court as well as Meet-the-Dolphin where you can feel a dolphin.

Harry: When are you going to take us there?

Porter: I will bring you guys on tour to Singapore next summer camp.

Ⅱ. New Words and Expressions

1. Singapore [ˌsɪŋəˈpɔː] n. 新加坡
2. city state n. 城邦国家;城市国家
3. Alexander the Great n. 亚历山大大帝
4. percent [pəˈsent] n.& adj. 百分比;百分之……的
5. mandarin [ˈmændərɪn] n. 普通话
6. Cantonese [ˌkæntəˈniːz, -ˈnɪs] n. 广东人;广东话
7. Malay [məˈleɪ] n. 马来人;马来语
8. official [əˈfɪʃl] adj.& n. 官方的;正式的;官员(文官)
9. language [ˈlæŋɡwɪdʒ] n. 语言;文字
10. government [ˈɡʌvənmənt] n. 政府;政体
11. common [ˈkɒmən] adj. 普通的;通俗的
12. education [ˌedʒuˈkeɪʃn] n. 教育;教育学
13. highlight [ˈhaɪlaɪt] n. 最重要部分;最精彩部分
14. Sentosa n. 〈地名〉圣淘沙(新加坡)
15. court [kɔːt] n. 球场;院落;宫廷
16. dolphin [ˈdɒlfɪn] n. 海豚
17. on tour to 漫游中;周游或巡回中

Ⅲ. Exercises

Answer the following questions according to the dialogue:

1. What does Singapore mean?
2. How many languages do people speak in Lion City?
3. What can you do there in Sentosa, the city state?
4. Suppose you are on a summer camp tour to Singapore, please make aspecific plan for a three-day visit.

Lesson 24 A Visit to the Bali Island

★ Sundowners are enjoying the sea views at Klapa, Bali Isand, Indonesia.

Background Information

Bali is a popular tourist destination, which has seen a significant rise in tourists since the 1980s. Tourism-related business makes up 80% of its economy. It is renowned for its highly developed arts, including traditional and modern dance, sculpture, painting, leather, metalworking, and music.

Bali Island is the Indonesia-famous tourist area. Because this island situated in the tropic zone, and the sea influence on climate temperature, the soil is extremely fertile. Green mountains and clean waters are here and there with tens of thousands of brilliant flowers. The forest is towering.

The local people use the flowers to decorate their city everywhere, therefore, this island's nickname is called "Island of the Flowers" and "the Paradise Island". The inhabitants on Bali Island hold every year religious holiday. Each time the people meet the holiday with songs and dance. Once you step in the soil of the island, you will be able to experience the exotic flavours that you never did before.

Lesson 24 A Visit to the Bali Island

Ⅰ. Dialogue

Harry: When was your last visit to the Bali Island?

Porter: Two years ago, but it seems to me that happened yesterday.

Harry: Good to hear that. The sands are nice and I like the beach weather very much. The sea view is just so impressive.

Porter: Did you go diving into the sea?

Harry: Absolutely yes. It's a must of your itinerary once you are in the Bali Island. The world under the sea is so beautiful and attractive.

Porter: How do you enjoy your diving experience?

Harry: Well, awesome! They trained me for about ten minutes and I learned how to use a scuba. And I become a frogman.

Porter: What did you see under the water?

Harry: Wow! It's a thrilling world. Much more beautiful than any of the aquariums that I have ever seen. I saw star fish, sea dog, and colorful corals, etc. Anyway, it is a very different world.

Porter: Anything else you like there?

Harry: Let me see. Oh, the spa is pretty good, especially, after a busy day.

Porter: Sure. It must be a good relaxation. A full body massage will make you feel good. I hear they use python to help.

Harry: Did you enjoy the durian while your stay in the Bali Island?

Porter: It smells bad, but after I saw many people eat it. I had a try and it was really yummy. It's always a good idea to start something new.

Ⅱ. New Words and Expressions

1. seem [si:m] v. 似乎；仿佛

2. beach [bi:tʃ] n. 海滩；海滨

3. weather ['weðə(r)] n. 天气；气象

4. dive [daɪv] *vi.* 潜水；跳水

5. itinerary [aɪˈtɪnərəri] *n.* 旅行日程；路线

6. experience [ɪkˈspɪərɪəns] *n.* 经验；经历

7. train [treɪn] *vt.& vi.* 训练；培养

8. minute [ˈmɪnɪt] *n.* 分；分钟

9. scuba [ˈskjuːbə] *n.* 水肺；便携式水下呼吸器

10. aquarium [əˈkweərɪəm] *n.* 水族馆；养鱼缸

11. colorful [ˈkʌləfəl] *adj.* 鲜艳的；多姿多彩的

12. coral [ˈkɒrəl] *n.* 珊瑚；珊瑚虫

13. anyway [ˈenɪweɪ] *adv.* 不论以何种方式；无论如何

14. spa [spɑː] *n.* 休闲健身中心；矿泉疗养地

15. especially [ɪˈspeʃəli] *adv.* 尤其地；主要地

16. massage [ˈmæsɑːʒ] *n.* 按摩；推拿

17. python [ˈpaɪθən] *n.* 蟒蛇

18. durian [ˈduərɪən] *n.* （马来群岛产的）榴莲果；榴莲树

19. smell [smel] *vt.& vi.* 闻；闻出

20. a must of 必做的事

Ⅲ. Exercises

Answer the following questions according to the dialogue：

1. Please tell us the location of Bali Island and its weather.

2. Did you dive into sea with a scuba? Tell us how.

3. Have you been to the Ocean World?

4. What can people see under the water? What marine products and seabed are there under the water?

(Keywords：edible seaweed, kelp, undersea mining, green turtle, hot pepper, aquamarine, conch, sea horse, conger pike, dried shrimps, sea catfish, sea cow, sea pen, sea cucumber, dolphin, sea food, sea crab, date palm, jellyfish, sea fish, fur seal, sea salt, marine animal ...)

Lesson 25　ASEAN

★ ASEAN and China are on good terms and "10 + 1" maximize the strength of both sides.

Background Information

Regional organizations (ROs) are, in a sense, international organizations (IOs), as they incorporate international membership and encompass geopolitical entities that operationally transcend a single nation state. However, their membership is characterized by boundaries and demarcations characteristic to a defined and unique geography, such as continents, or geopolitics, such as economic blocs. They have been established to foster cooperation and political and economic integration or dialogue amongst states or entities within a restrictive geographical or geopolitical boundary. They both reflect common patterns of development and history that have been fostered since the end of World War II as well as the fragmentation inherent in globalization. Most ROs tend to work alongside well-established multilateral organizations such as the United Nations. In many instances, a regional organization is simply referred to as an international organization, while in many others it makes sense to use the term regional organization to stress the more limited scope of a particular membership.

Examples of ROs include AU, EU, CARICOM, AL, ASEAN, SAARC, USAN, etc.

Lesson 25 ASEAN

Ⅰ. Text

The Association of Southeast Asian Nations, or ASEAN, was established on 8 August 1967 in Bangkok, Thailand, with the signing of the ASEAN Declaration (Bangkok Declaration) by the Founding Fathers of ASEAN, namely Indonesia, Malaysia, Philippines, Singapore and Thailand.

Brunei Darussalam, Viet Nam, Lao PDR, Myanmar and Cambodia then joined ASEAN, making up what is today the ten Member States of ASEAN.

The ASEAN Secretariat was set up in February 1976 by the Foreign Ministers of ASEAN. It was then housed at the Department of Foreign Affairs of Indonesia in Jakarta.

The Secretary-General of ASEAN is appointed by the ASEAN Summit for a non-renewable term of office of five years, selected from among nationals of the ASEAN Member States based on alphabetical rotation.

The ASEAN Charter serves as a firm foundation in achieving the ASEAN Community by providing legal status and institutional framework for ASEAN. It also codifies ASEAN norms, rules and values; sets clear targets for ASEAN; and presents accountability and compliance.

Since the process began in 1997, ASEAN Plus Three (APT) cooperation has broadened and deepened. It includes cooperation in the areas of political and security, transnational crime, economic, finance, tourism, agriculture and forestry, energy, minerals, small and medium-sized enterprises, environment, rural development and poverty eradication, social welfare, youth, women, civil service, labour, culture and arts, information and media, education, science, technology & innovation and public health.

Ⅱ. New Words and Expressions

1. association [əˌsəʊʃɪˈeɪʃn] n. 协会；社团；联合；联系
2. establish [ɪˈstæblɪʃ] vt. 建立；创建；确立或使安全

3. declaration [ˌdeklə'reɪʃn] n. 宣言；(纳税品在海关的)申报

4. founding ['faʊndɪŋ] n. 创始；建造

5. secretariat [ˌsekrə'teərɪət] n. 秘书处；书记处；秘书之职

6. Secretary-General ['sekrətrɪ 'dʒenərəl] n. 秘书长；总书记

7. appoint [ə'pɔɪnt] vt. 任命；委派；约定；指定；装设；布置

8. summit ['sʌmɪt] n. 顶点；高层会议；最高阶层

9. non-renewable [ˌnɒn rɪ'njuːəbl] adj. 不可再生的；不可更新的

10. select [sɪ'lekt] vt. 选择；挑选；选拔

11. alphabetical [ˌælfə'betɪkl] adj. 按字母(表)顺序的

12. rotation [rəʊ'teɪʃn] n. 旋转；轮流；循环

13. legal status n. 法律地位

14. codify ['kəʊdɪfaɪ] vt. 把(法律)编成法典；编成法典

15. norms [nɔːms] n. 标准；规范；准则；行为模式

16. accountability [əˌkaʊntə'bɪlɪtɪ] n. 有责任；可计量性

17. compliance [kəm'plaɪəns] n. 服从；承诺

18. cooperation [kəʊˌɒpə'reɪʃn] n. 合作；协作；协助；配合

19. transnational crime n. 跨国犯罪

20. enterprise ['entəpraɪz] n. 企(事)业单位；事业心；进取心

21. eradication [ɪˌrædɪ'keɪʃn] n. 摧毁，根除

Ⅲ. Exercises

Answer the following questions according to the text:

1. What does ASEAN stand for? When and where was the organization established?

2. When was the ASEAN Secretariat set up and where was it housed?

3. How much do you know about the ASEAN Charter? Give us some details and explain.

4. What is "10＋3"? Pick out one or two cooperation areas that you are familiar with and give us some examples to explain.

Lesson 26　Turkey: the Crossroad of East and West

★ A bridge spans the Bosphorus Strait linking up the two continents of Europe and Asia.

Background Information

The Republic of Turkey is a parliamentary republic largely located in Western Asia with the portion of Eastern Thrace in Southeastern Europe. Turkey is bordered by eight countries. The Mediterranean Sea is to the south, the Aegean Sea to the west, and the Black Sea to the north.

Turkey is a member of the UN, NATO, OECD, OSCE, OIC and the G20. After becoming one of the first members of the Council of Europe in 1949, Turkey became an associate member of the EEC in 1963, joined the EU Customs Union in 1995 and started full membership negotiations with the European Union in 2005. Turkey's growing economy and diplomatic initiatives have led to its recognition as a regional power.

It is worth mentioning that Istanbul was the capital of East Rome when Roman Empire split up. Today this country is important to China's strategy of the Belt and Road.

Lesson 26 Turkey: the Crossroad of East and West

Ⅰ. Text

When we talk about turkey, we think about Christmas Eve or Thanksgiving Day. Many people know that turkey is a big bird on the farm for meat. But what we are speaking about here is a country called Turkey on the Mediterranean Sea. Turkey's location at the crossroads of Europe and Asia makes it a country of great importance.

In Turkey, the number of people who believe in Muslin takes up 99%. Still, there are about 120,000 people believe in Christianity including some 85,000 Orthodox, 35,000 Roman Catholics, and smaller numbers of Protestants. Today, there are 236 churches open for worship in Turkey.

Istanbul is the largest city of Turkey, formerly called Byzantium and later Constantinople. In 324, Constantine Ⅰ made Byzantium the new capital of the Roman Empire, renaming it New Rome.

Troy is the place known for the Trojan War. So famous a war that they named a computer virus after the Troy and called it Trojan. The city of Troy attracts many tourists on daily basis.

By the way, the Ottoman Empire was very strong. In the sixteenth and seventeenth centuries, the Ottoman Empire was one of the world's great powers.

To go or not to go, that is the question.

Ⅱ. New Words and Expressions

1. turkey ['tɜːkɪ] n. 火鸡;火鸡肉;土耳其(首字母大写)
2. crossroad ['krɔːsrəʊd] n. 十字路口;重大抉择的关头
3. farm [fɑːm] n. 农场;农庄
4. meat [miːt] n. 肉;食物
5. location [ləʊ'keɪʃn] n. 位置;场所
6. importance [ɪm'pɔːtns] n. 重要性;重要地位
7. still [stɪl] adv. 仍;仍然

8. including [ɪnˈkluːdɪŋ] v. 包括(include 的现在分词);包含

9. church [tʃɜːtʃ] n. [宗]教堂;[宗]教徒;[宗]教派;[宗]教会

10. Istanbul [ˌɪstænˈbuːl] n. 伊斯坦布尔(土耳其西北部港市)

11. formerly [ˈfɔːməli] adv. 原来;以前

12. Byzantium [bɪˈzæntɪəm] n. 拜占庭(伊斯坦布尔的旧称)

13. Constantinople [ˌkɒnstæntɪˈnəʊpl] n. 君士坦丁堡(伊斯坦布尔)

14. rename [ˌriːˈneɪm] vt. 给……重新取名;改名

15. Ottoman [ˈɒtəmən] adj. 奥斯曼土耳其帝国的;土耳其人的

16. century [ˈsentʃəri] n. 百年;一世纪

17. Troy [trɔɪ] n. 〈地名〉特洛伊(土耳其)

18. Trojan [ˈtrəʊdʒən] n. 特洛伊

19. war [wɔː(r)] n. 战争;战争期间

Ⅲ. Exercises

Answer the following questions according to the text:

1. Where is Turkey? Why do you think the country is important?

2. What are the religions there? Can you describe the religious situation?

3. Would you make a briefing on the history of Istanbul?

4. Please kindly describe the Trojan War in groups.

Lesson 27 Mysterious Dubai

★ The best hotel in the world lies on the coast of Dubai, UAE.

Background Information

Dubai used to be a small fishing village, like China's southeast city of Shenzhen. But it develops much faster than Shenzhen, thanks to the contribution of oil. It is a very internationalized city not only in the United Arab Emirates but the whole world. Being the center of economy and finance in the Middle East, Dubai enjoys a very high prestige in the world.

High rises and skyscrapers have been built lately, among which the Khalifa Tower tops the world. The revitalization of the Arab world can be captured more or less here in the six Emirates.

People in Dubai have successfully made impossible possible. They are confident to establish their homeland into a paradise. Hopefully a new Tower of Babel is to be reconstructed.

The exotic architectures, sands-surfing, bazzar and barbecue are really impressive and a time to remember.

Lesson 27 Mysterious Dubai

Ⅰ. Dialogue

Harry: I hear Dubai is a city-state like Singapore.

Porter: Nope. Dubai is one of the emirates in the UAE. It used to be a small fishing village and was pretty poor before the oil was found. Today, it is an international city on desert.

Harry: What can you do at the oasis? I mean the small area in a desert where water and plants are found.

Porter: You can do a lot of things there. Many people go there to see "Khalifa Tower", which is a skyscraper in Dubai and is the tallest building in the world with a height of 829.8 meters.

Harry: What are the most attractive things there?

Porter: Well, Burj Al Arab hotel is the only 7-star hotel in the world. Afternoon tea or cocktails may be interesting.

Harry: Unluckily, I was not able to use the room service, but I could pay for lunch or dinner there. And buffet is 120 US dollars per person. There is a huge variety of raw materials for cooking and a la carte is the menu for VIP.

Porter: I hear that they are very ambitious and make a palm island in the sea, right?

Harry: You are right. The land reclamation is on a large scale. They plan to make three palm islands. These largest man-made islands in the world are along the coast of the Persian Gulf.

Porter: And each of the islands is shaped like a palm tree with a trunk connecting to the mainland. The branch of the tree is in the shape of a crescent moon where many people can live on.

Ⅱ. New Words and Expressions

1. used to 过去时常；过去曾(而现在不再)做
2. oil [ɔil] n. 油；石油；油画

3. desert ['dezət] n. 沙漠；荒地
4. oasis [əʊ'eɪsɪs] n. (沙漠中的)绿洲
5. tower ['taʊə(r)] n. 塔
6. skyscraper ['skaɪskreɪpə(r)] n. 摩天大楼
7. height [haɪt] n. 高度；海拔
8. attractive [ə'træktɪv] adj. 有魅力的；引人注目的
9. hotel [həʊ'tel] n. 旅馆；宾馆
10. cocktail ['kɒkteɪl] n. 鸡尾酒
11. buffet ['bʊfeɪ] n. 自助餐
12. dollar ['dɒlə(r)] n. 美元
13. palm [pɑːm] n. (象征胜利的)棕榈叶；棕榈树
14. island ['aɪlənd] n. 岛；岛屿
15. shape [ʃeɪp] n. 形状；状态 vt. 塑造；使符合
16. leaf [liːf] n. 叶子；页
17. trunk [trʌŋk] n. 树干；象鼻；躯干
18. connect [kə'nekt] vt. 连接；联结
19. mainland ['meɪnlænd] n. 大陆；本土
20. crescent ['kresnt] n. 新月；月牙

Ⅲ. Exercises

Answer the following questions according to the dialogue：

1. What are the differences between Dubai today and Dubai yesterday?
2. What are the most attractive things in Dubai?
3. What is the meaning of "a palm island"? Could you describe what a palm island in Dubai looks like?
4. How much do you know about Dubai?

Lesson 28 League of Arab States

★ What is the future for the peoples in the Arab world?

Background Information

The Arab League, formally, the League of Arab States, is a regional organization of Arab countries in and around North Africa, the Horn of Africa and Arabia. It was formed in Cairo on 22 March 1945 with six members: Kingdom of Egypt, Kingdom of Iraq, Transjordan (renamed Jordan in 1949), Lebanon, Saudi Arabia, and Syria. Yemen joined as a member on 5 May 1945. Currently, the League has 22 members, although Syria's participation has been suspended since November 2011, as a consequence of government repression during the ongoing uprising and civil war.

The League's main goal is to "draw closer the relations between member States and co-ordinate collaboration between them, to safeguard their independence and sovereignty, and to consider in a general way the affairs and interests of the Arab countries".

Early in 1953, ties between China and Arab League have been established and it was in 1993, League of Arab countries set up its office in Beijing, hence the exchanges of visits are on the regular basis. In this way, both China and members of Arab League benefit from one another in many areas.

Lesson 28 League of Arab States

I. Text

The land of the Arab League is mostly covered with sands, but the oases allow the people there to live a good life. Members of the League of Arab States cover a large part of the Muslim world, if not all of it. Iran, Malaysia and Indonesia are not included at least, these countries are exceptions rather than the rules.

As Samuel Huntington, a Harvard professor, described in his book called *Clash of Civilization* that the human civilizations include Western, Confucian, Japanese, Islamic, Hindu, Slavic-Orthodox, Latin American and possibly African civilization.

Mr. Prof, we think it is only his own opinion, concluded in the book that the Islam conflicts with all its surrounding civilizations, therefore members of the Arab League are trouble makers. In his eyes, the conflicts and violence even occur between members states and groups within the Arab world.

We find the view of the book unfair to the Arab League. Historically, links between China and Arab world had been built thanks to the Silk Road. We have much in common and we believe this ancient road will strengthen the bilateral relations between two sides with China's Belt and Road Initiative.

It is known to all that people there don't have much land to till, but they have oil under. China needs oil from that region and the Arab League needs manufactured products from China. The trade between the two areas is highly complementary. We are very interdependent. More cooperation and less zero-sum game will help stabilize the world. And all these exchanges have already reactivated and will continue to revitalize the Silk Road.

In 1993, Arab League has set up its office in Beijing to better the connections. Last year, China-Arab States Expo Online Silk Road Forum is sponsored by the Chinese government. All these mean the bilateral relations will flourish.

China's peaceful rise needs a harmonious international community.

Ⅱ. New Words and Expressions

1. Arab ['ærəb] adj. 阿拉伯的;阿拉伯人的;阿拉伯语的
2. league [li:g] n. 联盟;同盟
3. Muslim ['mʊzlɪm] adj. 穆斯林;穆斯林的
4. describe [dɪ'skraɪb] vt. 描写;形容;叙述;作图
5. Islamic [ɪz'læmɪk] adj. 伊斯兰的;伊斯兰教的
6. Hindu ['hɪndu:] adj. 印度教的;印度人的
7. Slavic-Orthodox ['sla:vɪk 'ɔ:θədɒks] n. 斯拉夫东正教
8. conclude [kən'klu:d] vt.& vi. 得出结论;缔结;推断出
9. conflict ['kɒnflɪkt] n. 冲突;战斗;矛盾
10. violence ['vaɪələns] n. 暴力;暴虐;猛烈;激烈
11. strengthen ['streŋθn] n.& vi. 加强;巩固;勉励;激励
12. till [tɪl] vt. 耕种;耕地
13. region ['ri:dʒən] n. 地区;行政区;(学问等的)范围;领域
14. complementary [ˌkɒmplɪ'mentrɪ] adj. 互补的;补充的
15. interdependent [ˌɪntədɪ'pendənt] adj. 互相依存的
16. zero-sum game n. 零和游戏
17. stabilize ['steɪbəlaɪz] vt.& vi. (使)稳定;使稳定平衡
18. reactivate [rɪ'æktɪveɪt] vt. 使恢复活动;重起作用
19. revitalize [ˌri:'vaɪtəlaɪz] vt. 使恢复元气;使新生;使复兴
20. expo ['ekspəʊ] = exposition n. 〈非正〉博览会;展览会
21. forum ['fɔ:rəm] n. 论坛;讨论会;专题讨论节目
22. sponsor ['spɒnsə(r)] n. 发起者;主办者 vt. 赞助
23. bilateral [ˌbaɪ'lætərəl] adj. 双边的;两侧的;双向的
24. flourish ['flʌrɪʃ] vt.& vi. 茂盛;繁荣;活跃
25. harmonious [hɑ:'məʊnɪəs] adj. 和谐的;融洽的;协调的

Lesson 28 League of Arab States

III. Exercises

Answer the following questions according to the text:

1. Where is the head office of the League of Arab States? How many member states in the league and who are they?
2. What is the main ideas of Hunting's *Clash of Civilization*? How do you look at it?
3. How much do you know about the Silk Road? Give us some details and explain.
4. How is China related to Arab world? Give us some examples that you are familiar with to explain.

Lesson 29 Moonlighting

★ Moonlight means to get a part time job. And many college students studying abroad may have the experience of moonlighting.

Lesson 29 Moonlighting

Background Information

In job application, interview is often the decisive factor in getting a position. It is designed to find out more about an applicant and to see if one is suitable for a particular job. So if one is lucky enough to be called for an interview, good preparation beforehand is necessary. Find out as much as possible about the job and consider how one's qualifications and experience can be related to it.

As an international student studying abroad, you are expected to be independent like other local students.

Normally, your school will provide you with a lot of on campus job opportunities like teaching assistant or lab assistant. Students can also choose to work off campus to earn more money, but remember each particular country has its own policy for part-time job hours even each state varies.

No matter you work on-campus or off-campus, the job opening must be legal and security matters.

It is worth mentioning that you are expected to give priority to learn how to cook and cut the hair before you study abroad, and it can save you a lot of money.

Ⅰ. Dialogue

Harry: Have a seat please. Mr. Porter. Let me take a quick look at your application ... I see that you want a part-time job, right?

Porter: That's right. And I am an international student here.

Harry: We hire part-timers occasionally. How many hours a week do you want to work?

Porter: About fifteen or twenty something.

Harry: You're a junior at the university. Also, you were a lifeguard for the past two summers for the swimming club.

Porter: Yes. But this year I have an apartment. Therefore I need a job to pay for the rents.

Harry: Do you think you can handle both a job and school?

Porter: Well, I have a B average. I think I can do it.

Harry: Your track record is very good. They say you're a hard worker and very reliable ...

Porter: I seldom miss work, and I'm always on time.

Harry: Well, Porter, we have one opening now.

Porter: That's wonderful!

Harry: Well, we are a logistic company and need a clerk in the mail room. The job pays the minimum wage. However, It's on the night shift.

Porter: That's fine. And it fits me well.

Harry: The hours are 2 to 6 am, Monday through Friday.

Porter: That's ... not so good. I'm an early bird but not that early.

Harry: I know. What do you think? Are you interested in?

Porter: Well, I often take a catnap in the afternoon, and then I stay up late. I guess the hours are okay. When do I start?

Harry: On Monday.

Porter: Deal. Thanks a bunch.

Lesson 29 Moonlighting

Ⅱ. New Words and Expressions

1. moonlight ['mu:nlaɪt] v. 兼职
2. application [ˌæplɪ'keɪʃn] n. 申请书；申请表
3. part-time [pɑːt taɪm] n. 业余时间；兼职的
4. hire ['haɪə(r)] v. 雇用
5. lifeguard ['laɪfgɑːd] n. 救生员
6. club [klʌb] n. 俱乐部
7. apartment [ə'pɑːtmənt] = flat n. 公寓
8. handle ['hændl] v. 处理；解决
9. average ['ævərɪdʒ] n.& adj. 平均；平均的；普通的
10. track record n. 简历；信用记录
11. reliable [rɪ'laɪəbl] adj. 可靠的；确实的
12. mailroom ['meɪlruːm] n. 邮件舱；邮件收发室
13. clerk [klɑːk] n. 职员
14. minimum ['mɪnɪməm] adj. 最小的；最少量
15. shift [ʃɪft] n. 轮班；更换
16. guess [ges] v. 猜测
17. on the night shift 上夜班
18. catnap ['kætnæp] n. 打盹
19. stay up 熬夜

Ⅲ. Exercises

Answer the following questions according to the dialogue：

1. What is international student? How many hours are they allowed to work as a part-timer?
2. Why does Porter choose a night shift to moonlight?
3. What are the reasons that so many students study abroad?

Lesson 30 South Africa

★ Cape of Good Hope in Capetown, South Africa, the dividing point of both Atlantic and Indian Ocean.

Background Information

South Africa is located at the Southern tip of African continent and is one of BRICS members now. It has three capitals with Tshwane (used to be called Pretoria) as its administrative capital, Capetown as its seat of legislation and Bloemfontein as its justice center.

Surrounded by the Atlantic and Indian Ocean, black people were driven away from west coast to east coast by the white people. Therefore, more white people in the west coast and more black people in the east coast while more colored people in the middle.

Johannesburg is the largest city and economic center in the country. Although apartheid or segregation are overshadowed, people can see and feel the racial discrimination. Colored people are still struggling for their legitimate rights.

With the appearance of the first black president, South African economy is flourishing. Gold mining and diamond process are the main industry there.

South Africa used to be the colony of western powers. Dutch, German and English have visited the country. The official language is Afrikaans, which is a mixture of Dutch, German and English.

Ⅰ. Text

South Africa is a country in the southern part of African continent. Indian Ocean is to its east and Atlantic Ocean to its west. It has three capitals, which is very different from China. White people and colored people as well as the black people are living together now. The apartheid or racial segregation is gone, gone with the wind.

Some people come to the country for gold and diamond which are very expensive. Other people come here for wildlife such as lion, rhino, baboon, giraffe, elephant, etc. Anyway, South Africa is a beautiful land with nice people and rich natural resources.

Diamond is a kind of hard stone. So hard that people say, "Diamonds cut diamonds". You can see a lot of diamonds in the Chinese market but mostly are processed in South Africa. Visitors will also see more things there like ostrich egg, abalone and so on.

Today, the white-only days are over, and Nelson Mandela became South Africa's first black president and won the Nobel Peace Prize in 1993. More and more tourists are flocking into the land and the Cape of Good Hope is a must on the schedule. And Table Mountain is on the top list of New 7 Wonders of the World.

With a population of more than 50 million, it's an important member of BRICS. South Africa was poor yesterday but is a star today. We believe it will be a prosperous country tomorrow.

Ⅱ. New Words and Expressions

1. ocean [ˈəʊʃn] *n.* 洋；海洋

2. Atlantic [ætˈlæntɪk] *adj.* 在大西洋里的，近大西洋的

3. apartheid [əˈpɑːtaɪt] *n.* （以往南非的）种族隔离制度

4. diamond [ˈdaɪəmənd] *n.* 钻石，金刚石；菱形

5. rhino [ˈraɪnəʊ] *n.* 犀牛

6. baboon [bæˈbuːn] n. 狒狒

7. anyway [ˈenɪˌweɪ] adv. 不论以何种方法；无论如何

8. resource [rɪˈsɔːs] n. 资源；物力，财力

9. process [ˈprəuses] n.& v. 过程；程序；加工；生产

10. ostrich [ˈɒstrɪtʃ] n. 鸵鸟；逃避现实的人

11. abalone [ˌæbəˈləunɪ] n. 〈美〉鲍鱼

12. expensive [ɪkˈspensɪv] adj. 昂贵的；价格高的

13. wildlife [ˈwaɪldlaɪf] n. 野生动物

14. a kind of 一种；一类

15. flock [flɒk] v.& n. 成群活动；兽群

16. cape [keɪp] n. 海角；岬

17. prosperous [ˈprɒsp(ə)rəs] adj. 繁荣的；兴旺的

Ⅲ. Exercises

Answer the following questions according to your knowledge：

1. Can you say something about South Africa? How much do you know about the Big Fives?

2. What makes South Africa famous in the world?

3. What does BRICS stand for? Why is South Africa an important member of the BRICS?

4. Where is Cape Town in South Africa? What is the true meaning of the Cape of Good Hope?

Lesson 31: Namibia: the Youngest Country in Africa

★ The author met with a high ranking official of Namibia in Windhoek.

Lesson 31 Namibia: the Youngest Country in Africa

Background Information

Namibia, formerly German South-West Africa and then South West Africa, is a country in southern Africa whose western border is the Atlantic Ocean. It gained independence from South Africa on 21 March 1990, following the Namibian War of Independence.

The dry lands of Namibia were inhabited since early times by San, Damara, and Namaqua, and since about the 14th century A.D. by immigrating Bantu who came with the Bantu expansion. Most of the territory became a German Imperial protectorate in 1884.

Agriculture, herding, tourism and the mining industry — including mining for gem diamonds, uranium, gold, silver, and base metals form the basis of Namibia's economy.

Historically, the country experienced periods of Pre-colonial period, German rule, South African rule and After independence. Since its independence, Namibia has completed the transition from white minority apartheid rule to parliamentary democracy.

I. Dialogue

Harry: How's your trip to Namibia? Must be thrilling!

Porter: Well, it was a tiring journey and the jet-lag was bad but it's worthwhile to see so many dunes and wild lives.

Harry: What's your itinerary then?

Porter: Cool. We flew from Shanghai via Qatar and Johannesburg to Windhoek, the capital of Namibia.

Harry: How was your flight?

Porter: We checked in at the Shanghai International Airport and we chose to go through the green channel of the customs because we have nothing to declare. After the passport control we began to board the plane and we love the cabin. Very soon the plane started to taxi and took off. Anyway, it was a beautiful flight and landing with no air turbulence. The captain and crew were terrific too.

Harry: How do you like your stay in Namibia? What's your impression on that young country?

Porter: Our delegation was warmly welcomed by Her Excellency, the woman governor of Khomas province. Talks were held on the bilateral relations and co-operations in various areas including the students exchange programs. It was a fruitful visit with memos signed.

Harry: I hear 80% of Namibia's daily necessities were imported from South Africa. Is there any possibility for China to join the market?

Porter: Good question. Ties between China and Namibia are an important part of Sino-African friendships. China's excess capacity of industry is seeking business opportunity in Namibia. Part of the missions of this visit is to expand our market.

Harry: Anything else to share?

Porter: The air is fresh and the sky is exceptionally blue, no haze, no smog, no pollution or contamination. People are friendly and biz opportunities are huge. And you can perceive the German existence along the Atlantic Coast, particularly the dark beer.

Harry: How about the investment environment?

Porter: Cool. A good number of the Chinese companies have set up their branches in Namibia and their legitimate interests are well protected by the local government. And ROI is rewarding.

Ⅱ. New Words and Expressions

1. thrilling ['θrɪlɪŋ] *adj.* 刺激的;惊悚的
2. leg [leg] *n.* 一段飞行;腿
3. jet-lag ['dʒet læg] *n.* 时差;时差综合征
4. dune [djuːn] *n.* (风吹形成的)沙丘
5. check in 交运行李
6. customs ['kʌstəmz] *n.* 海关;习惯(custom 的名词复数)
7. declare [dɪ'kleə] *v.* 申报;宣誓
8. cabin ['kæbɪn] *n.* 机舱;船舱
9. landing ['lændɪŋ] *n.* 落地;降落
10. turbulence ['tɜːbjʊləns] *n.* 气流;气旋
11. captain & crew *n.* 机长和乘务人员
12. delegation [ˌdelɪ'ɡeɪʃn] *n.* 代表;授权
13. Her Excellency *n.* 阁下
14. bilateral [ˌbaɪ'lætərəl] *adj.* 双边的;双方的
15. memo ['meməʊ] *n.* 备忘录
16. daily necessities *n.* 日用品
17. Sino- ['saɪnəʊ] *adj.* 中国的;中国与……的;中……的
18. expand [ɪk'spænd] *v.* 拓展;延伸
19. exceptionally [ɪk'sepʃənəli] *adv.* 非常地;格外地
20. contamination [kənˌtæmɪ'neɪʃn] *n.* 污染

21. perceive ［pə'siːv］ v. 察觉；理解；明白

22. investment ［ɪn'vestmənt］ n. 投资；投资额

23. branch ［brɑːntʃ］ n. 分支；枝叶

24. legitimate ［lɪ'dʒɪtɪmət］ adj. 合理的；合法的

25. protect ［prə'tekt］ v. 保护

26. ROI = Return on Investment 投资回报

Ⅲ. Exercises

Answer the following questions according to the dialogue：

1. What's the itinerary for the delegation?
2. What is the normal procedure for stepping into the soil of another country? Describe it in the class as much as you can.
3. What did the delegation do in Namibia?
4. How much do you know about the Republic of Namibia?

Lesson 32 Shanghai Cooperation Organization

Lesson 32 — Shanghai Cooperation Organization

★ A night view of Shanghai, the oriental financial center of the Far East.

Background Information

The Shanghai Cooperation Organisation is a Eurasian political, economic and military organisation which was founded in 2001 in Shanghai by the leaders of China, Kazakhstan, Kyrgyzstan, Russia, Tajikistan, and Uzbekistan. These countries, except Uzbekistan, had been members of the Shanghai Five, founded in 1996. After the inclusion of Uzbekistan in 2001, the members renamed the organisation. On July 10, 2015, the SCO decided to admit India and Pakistan as full members.

Except for Afghanistan, the observers are moving towards being accorded full member status. Meanwhile, in 2012, Armenia, Azerbaijan, Bangladesh, Belarus, Nepal and Sri Lanka applied for observer status within the organization. Syria has also submitted an application for observer status, while Egypt, Maldives and Ukraine have applied for dialogue partner status.

Lesson 32 Shanghai Cooperation Organization

I. Text

Shanghai Cooperation Organization follows the purposes of the United Nations. As a regional organization, its aim is to safeguard the security of its member states and all members support one another in cracking down the threat from outside. So far this non-aligned body has only six member states, but it is open to interested parties or countries in the rest of the world. We believe it will be a giant in the international community.

On July 10, 2015, the SCO decided to admit India and Pakistan as full members. Afghanistan, Belarus, Iran, Mongolia have observer status in the SCO. The position of Dialogue Partner was created in 2008 in accordance with the SCO Charter. Sri Lanka and Turkey were granted dialogue partner status in the SCO.

China'a foreign policies are primarily based on the Five Principles as:

1. Mutual respect for sovereignty and territorial integrity.
2. Mutual non-aggression.
3. Non-interference in each other's internal affairs.
4. Equality and mutual benefit.
5. Peaceful co-existence.

Basically, the good neighbor relations of the SCO are based on the Five Principles of Peaceful Co-existence, which enable people all over the world to see the important role China plays in the institution.

Over the past few years, the organization's activities have expanded to include increased military cooperation, intelligence sharing, and counter-terrorism.

It is worth mentioning that SCO, with its head office in Beijing, established a Regional Anti-Terrorist Structure (RATS), headquartered in Tashkent, Uzbekistan, is a permanent organ of the SCO which serves to promote cooperation of member states against the three evils of terrorism, separatism and extremism.

Ⅱ. New Words and Expressions

1. safeguard ['seɪfɡɑːd] v. 保卫；捍卫

2. crack down 采取措施；打击

3. threat [θret] n. 威胁；恐吓

4. align [ə'laɪn] v. 使结盟

5. body ['bɒdɪ] n. 团体；机构；物体；身体

6. party ['pɑːtɪ] n. （当事的）一方；党派；派对

7. Belarus [ˌbeləˈruːs] n. 白俄罗斯

8. status ['steɪtəs] n. 地位；身份

9. partner ['pɑːtnə(r)] n. 伙伴；合伙人

10. in accordance with 依照；与……一致

11. charter ['tʃɑːtə] n. 宪章；章程

12. principle ['prɪnsəpl] n. 原则；原理

13. mutual ['mjuːtʃuəl] adj. 相互的；双方的

14. sovereignty ['sɒvrəntɪ] n. 国家主权；君权

15. integrity [ɪn'teɡrətɪ] n. 完整；诚实；正直

16. aggression [ə'ɡreʃn] n. 攻击；侵略

17. interference [ˌɪntəˈfɪərəns] n. 干涉；打扰

18. internal [ɪn'tɜːnl] adj. 内部的；内政的

19. equality [ɪ'kwɒlətɪ] n. 同等；平等

20. benefit ['benɪfɪt] n. 利益；福祉

21. existence [ɪɡ'zɪstəns] n. 存在；存在物

22. institution [ˌɪnstɪ'tjuːʃn] n. 机构；团体

23. military ['mɪlətrɪ] adj. 军事的；军用的

24. counter-terrorism ['kaʊntə ˌterərɪzəm] n. 反恐怖主义

25. anti- ['æntɪ] adj. 反……

26. permanent ['pɜːmənənt] adj. 永久的；不变的

27. evil ['iːvl] adj. 邪恶的；有害的；品行坏的

Lesson 32　Shanghai Cooperation Organization

28. separatism ['seprətɪzəm] n. 分裂主义
29. extremism [ɪk'stri:mɪzəm] n. 极端主义

Ⅲ. Exercises

Answer the following questions according to the text:

1. What is the purpose of establishing the Shanghai Cooperation Organization?
2. What are the Five Principles of Peaceful Co-existence? Set an example to explain the importance of these principles.
3. Where is the head office of the SCO? Is it located in Shanghai or Beijing or Moscow?
4. Tell us about the history of the SCO in the class briefly and how much you know about this organization.